SOLITUDE
Image copyright © MicRo Images
Facebook: @microimagery

SUICIDE

A collection of poetry and short prose from writers around the world on the themes of suicide and self-harm

Compiled by Robin Barratt

With...

Abigail George, Barbara Hawthorn, Beaton Galafa, Bee Parkinson-Cameron, Bernadette Perez, Bill Cox, Chrys Salt, Cynthia Morrison, David A Banks, David Hollywood, David Lohrey, Donna Zephrine, Ebuwa Ohenhen, Eduard Schmidt-Zorner, Gabriella Garofalo, Guy Morris, Hannah Louise MacFarlane, Heera Nawaz, Ibn Qalam, Jo Wilson-Ridley, John Tunaley, John-Karl Stokes, Katrina Cattermole, Kimmy Alan, Linda M. Crate, LindaAnn LoSchiavo, Lynda Tavakoli, Malcolm Judd, Maliha Hassan, Margareth Stewart, Mark Blickley, Mary Anne Zammit, May Mathew Manoj, Michael J. Rollins, Mtende Wezi Nthara, Nikori Ese Praise, Nilanjana Bose, Noor Yousif, Nurah Harun, Pamela Scott, Parvinder Kaur, Pasithea Chan, Richard Goss, Robin Barratt, Sara Spivey, Sarah Clarke, Shereen Abraham, Sue Thomason, Trisha Lawty and Zahra Zuhair.

Published by Robin Barratt
ISBN: 9781091029347
© Robin Barratt and all the authors herein, 2019

W: www.RobinBarratt.co.uk
T: + 44 (0) 7508 833 433

www.SuicideTheBook.com

ABOUT ROBIN BARRATT

After a career in security, Robin is now an author, writer, publisher and poet. He started writing back in 2003, and is the genre best-selling author of six non-fiction true crime books, as well as a number of other books including one biography, two self-help guides and three anthologies about life and living in the Kingdom of Bahrain, where he lived for four years, and where he was also commissioned to produce and publish a quality book for the Kanoo family; one of the biggest Arab merchant families in the Gulf region. Robin also founded, edited and published the *Bahrain Arts Magazine*, the country's leading online arts platform, and compiled and published the acclaimed *Collections of Poetry and Prose* book series featuring almost 1400 pieces of work from 265 writers and poets from 49 countries around the world, all writing on particular topics and themes. Robin has also written articles for magazines and newspapers worldwide including; *Gulf Insider, Sur La Terre, Time Out, Norfolk* magazine, *Absolute Lifestyle, Signature, Exotic Car* and many more. He runs one-to-one creative writing and poetry workshops - both personally and online - and is in the process of setting up *Counselling Through Creativity,* a not-for-profit organisation helping and supporting others through the creative use of words as a effective, therapeutic tool for self-help and healing.

W: www.RobinBarratt.co.uk
FB: @RobinBarratt1
Instagram: @RobinBarratt1

"Be motivated to heal, be inspired to write."

COUNSELLING THROUGH CREATIVITY

All profits from the sale of this book will go towards the development of *Counselling Through Creativity,* a not-for-profit organisation helping and supporting others through the creative use of words as a effective, therapeutic tool for self-help and healing.

It is undeniable that putting your thoughts, feelings and emotions into words, on paper, either via a diary, poetry, song lyrics or in a short story format, can be an incredibly effective therapeutic and healing tool. *Counselling Through Creativity* inspires and motivates you to do exactly this. You can explore almost any subject; from suicidal thoughts and depression and feelings of low self-worth, to love, loneliness, betrayal... simply anything you'd like to write about! However, you do not have to be a writer or a poet, or to have written anything at all before; you just need to want to self-heal, and to use words as a way to help you do this.

And to motivate and inspire you even further, well-known authors, writers, song writers and poets will also talk about how they themselves use and have used words in a therapeutic and cathartic way, and will help you look at ways of how you can do the same. *Counselling Through Creativity* also plans to run free seminars and workshops (both live and online), and provide other creative based counselling, help and support.

SUPPORT COUNSELLING THROUGH CREATIVITY

Love words? Love motivating and inspiring people to write? Love helping people? Interested in promoting positive mental health? Then please contact *Counselling Through Creativity* if you are a company, group or organisation, or an individual interested in supporting and helping people creatively through the use of words.

www.CounsellingThroughCreativity.org

CONTENTS...

CONTENTS BY AUTHOR...

INTERVIEW PAGES:

Interviews can also be read online at:

www.suicidethebook.com/interviews/

SUICIDE

A collection of poetry and short prose from writers around the world on the themes of suicide and self-harm

MAROONED

By Hannah Louise MacFarlane

I feel it pressing against my cranium,
Like the barrel of a gun ready, loaded, locked.
A constant coldness on my temple,
That lies within an eternal promise,
To take my life.

It sits perched on a hill inside my mind,
Within the turntable that does not stop.
Spinning, stirring, and flashing,
In a constant loop that presents my failings,
Ready to win the fight.

I am no stranger to disappointment,
Pain is what fuels my drive, sparks my engine.
It is what makes it impossible to allow myself,
The bittersweet taste of failure,
Even once a while.

I am a prototype of half of a whole person,
A pick 'n mix of antidepressants and small rooms.
Clipboards, tissue boxes, flowers on the walls,
That are all designed to make me better,
But make me feel worse.

The blade was never once pleasing to me,
The harsh grey against my snow skin and blue veins.
It was the red that screamed of intense danger, pain,
The promise that came with those things,
The proof I was still alive.

It has been nothing short of a miracle,
That the blade has not crossed my skin in six hundred days.
Six hundred days since the last violent attack against myself,
Since I turned the water hues of red and pink,
Bleeding from my wrist intentionally.

That does not mean I am excited to live,
It simply means the demons inside my mind have been quiet.
Since I switched out blades for baskets of pens and notebooks.
Every time I want to cut my skin I write,
So instead of six hundred becoming zero, you read this, and I live.

ON A COLLEAGUE'S ATTEMPTED SUICIDE

By Sue Thomason

I was at fault, because I didn't know.
It took your life to bring it home to me.
I wish we could have talked it out, although
I never knew you well enough to see
The underclothing of your misery
crossing your heart beneath the public show.
Colleagues just don't discuss pain. We agree
to smile in corridors, to say "Hello,
how are you?" and move on, unhurriedly
forestalling answers. All of us are slow
to understand why we ignored you so;
we can't admit responsibility.
It took your life to bring it home to me:
I am at fault, because I wouldn't know.

Based on a co-worker's real and serious suicide attempt, which left several people in that work environment feeling confounded - we'd had no idea this person had been feeling so bad, and no idea of the pressure they were under outside work; their work performance hadn't fallen off at all. If there is a moral here it's; "Please talk. Please dare to speak the truth. Support can come from unexpected places."

THE PAIN THAT REMAINS

By Kimmy Alan

When you died that day
My life was painted in grey
In shades of self-blame

Suicide turns day
Into colours of dark rain
Forever in shame

If only I had known
What you were about to do
I could have stopped you

You may have passed on
But suicide inflicts pain
To us that remain

Whether family or first responders, a suicide leaves a legacy of pain to those you leave behind. Most torturous is the guilt that your loved one will feel, of what they could have done to help you. The shadow of your senseless act will follow them to the end of their days.

Interview with Kimmy

Who was it who took their life Kimmy?

The person that took her life was Katie, my neighbour, friend, confident and lover.

Can you tell me a little about Katie and how you met?

When I first met Katie, who was 15 years my junior, I was battling the rigours of chemo and radiation from my battle with stage 4 cancer. She had just moved into an apartment in the condo where I lived. Katie knocked on my door and introduced herself. She was beautiful and smart. I was old, hairless and looked like death warmed over. But Katie wasn't the slightest bit taken aback. In fact, she became an immediate friend who supported me in my cancer battle.

Though I found her very attractive, because of my age and my condition, I never considered our relationship to be anything more than plutonic. However, as I went into remission things changed and we became 'once and awhile' lovers and very close friends.

From the beginning I found Katie to be an extremely intelligent but complexed person. Thirty eight years of age, she had experienced a great deal of success that was followed by an unexpected devastating fall. Katie was the head of a mortgage company owned by a large bank. A graduate with a degree in math and business, she had a grasp for numbers that was almost savant. Looking back, Katie may have indeed been a savant. She had a large home and money in savings. All was good till the financial crash of 2008, when Katie along her entire department, were fired by her bank.

To say Katie was devastated is an understatement. Soon her savings were exhausted and she found herself unemployed and broke. She was emotionally and financially ruined. This fact, would always haunt us throughout our relationship.

Fast forward to 2017. Katie and I had an understanding. Though I enjoyed her company, because of our age difference and the fact I worried that my cancer might return, I encouraged Katie to see other men. Also, contributing to this understanding was that Katie had expressed to me that her biological clock was ticking. Because of this, and the fear that I would relapse, I encouraged her to move forward without me. She tried dating but things didn't work out. As a consequence Katie didn't have another man in her life. The important thing I must note, is that during this period I was experiencing some guilt, that I was an older man taking advantage of a young woman. So, though I was quite fond of her, I also never made any sort of commitment.

I loved Katie's company, but she was constantly expressed shame and regret over her financial demise. Often she slide into deep bouts of depression crying for hours at a time. It was trying but I became quite use to these unpleasant periods, so I endured till they passed. When suddenly, things turned much worse. Katie began to experience paranoid delusions. As a result, I would be in frequent contact with her parents who, like me, were extremely concerned. One particular night was so bad Katie wanted to barricade her door because 'they' were coming after her. I decided to call the police. I thought for certain the police would take Katie to a hospital for short-term treatment, but they couldn't, saying that under the law they couldn't do so unless she openly expressed the desire to harm herself. She hadn't.

For the next several months I and Katie's folks tried to convince her to seek help, but she refused. The last few weeks of her life Katie had lost her job and refused to speak to her family and friends, thinking they were part of a vast conspiracy that wanted to imprison her. Soon Katie refused to leave her apartment and wouldn't open the door for anyone. Finally, on one cold November morning, Katie did emerge from her apartment. She drove her car to a high bridge above the Mississippi River and threw herself into the frigid waters.

From this very moment I blamed myself for Katie's death believing that I could have done more to help her. Then I too, feel into a deep depression.

About a month after her death, Katie's father would confess to me a family secret. When Katie was a teen, she was diagnosed with mental illness. After receiving treatment, Katie went on to live a very productive life till she lost her job. Till the time of this revelation, I had blamed myself for Katie's death. I had believed that had I been more persuasive with the police, Katie could have gotten the help she so desperately need. Yet, what her father thought would be words of comfort only made me more troubled. Now, along with shame, anger was added to my grief. I went from asking myself; "what more could I have done," to "why didn't they tell me, so I could have done more?" I was so overwhelmed by thoughts of regret, I've been in therapy since.

Has therapy helped?

Yes, therapy has greatly benefited me. I've come to realize that, though I wished I had responded to her illness differently, the only one responsible for her death, was Katie herself. As a consequence I'm no longer angry at myself, Katie's parents, or the system that failed her. However, sometimes I find myself angry at Katie. If only she would have known the pain her death would cause others I doubt she would have taken her life. Granted, at the time of her death Katie had become completely delusional, but in the weeks leading up to it, she was cognitive enough to realize she need to allow us to get her help.

Have you learned anything from this tragedy?

Yes, from this tragedy I've learned couple of things;

First and foremost; no one should be ashamed to admit their struggle with mental illness. Though it still carries a stigma, the guiltiest people who perpetuate this, are those who keep their diagnosis a secret.

Second; there needs to be an awareness of the pain suicide causes others. Every time someone takes their own life, a ripple of hurt the echoes out in waves. Not only are family and friends impacted, but so are many innocent people as well. This includes the first responders who have to retrieve the body and the poor souls that often have to clean up the death scene. Though I extend my sympathy and understanding to anyone who contemplates suicide, they need to know, that to do so is a very selfish act that hurts many.

LIGHT, LESS HOIST

By David Hollywood

Struggle first to see the light,
Hurried, follow quickly, freedoms flight,
Strain, torn, empty, journeys task,
Chest strife's tussle, tight on grasp,
Remains thrashed anxious, by life's rasp,
Reveal cruel trials upon your way,
Lest time stops to say, you'll stay,
Best tempt afflications of your choice,
Case, throttled ideals don't delay,
Be then stymied by the hoist.

Left dangling lonely as you swing,
Drips, slowly leaves you, whilst it cease,
As all you yearned for was to sing,
Look down now low you, for your peace.

RED
By Parvinder Kaur

I don't remember why I did it for the very first time. I don't remember the second or even the third. It is very hard to recollect why or how you became a part of my life. To this day, even after you've been long gone, I can see you. I feel you. Each time my heart skips a beat, I know it's you moving in your grave. Banging against your coffin you try to break free from the bonds you had been tied in. You should have been dead by now. I had hammered your coffin with the strongest nails that I could get. I had prayed and pleaded to the sea, and she had her waves take you and bury you deep within her. But even after all of this, why do I still mourn you?

It was twistedly satisfying to let you completely control my body. I didn't have a to feel sadness in particular to come running back to you, the ghost of your presence lingered around the corner of every emotion. My fingers listened to you with extreme admiration. My wrist desperately begged for deep passionate kisses. My thighs were never satisfied and though the rest of me longed for the same touch, I just knew this affair had to be a secret.

I remember before I came to you for the last time, to see you off, to make sure that I was going to break this off, I sat down to have a little talk with myself. With my fingers, I traced the scars that you had left. To my wrist I gave quick, safe feeling kisses and to my thighs I showed pretty dresses that I could no longer wear because they landed right above where the remnants of our love had made a permanent home. I remember convincing them all, for a very brief moment, to listen to me and do what was right for all of us. And in that brief moment I remember picking you up, still sliver and exact but with a little rust around the corners from where I may not have cleaned my blood. I remember locking you away in a pretty pink box, rushing outside and disposing you off to where you were meant to be.

I remember my bath from that day very clearly, I remember feeling numb, I remember feeling alone and tired for days. I remember wanting to just touch you and I remember how bad I craved your touch. I wanted to feel you poke and cut through my skin. I wanted to feel you deep in my flesh. I wanted to see the red flow out and drip from my wrist to the drain, from my thigh to the drain. I wanted to flow with it into the drain, into the darkness and never return.

I don't remember how I saw the light again. I don't remember when I started going back to the kitchen and feeling nothing particular before picking up the knife. It looks very much like you and still reminds me of you. But that doesn't mean I want you to come back. I'm happier without you. I know I am in a better place and I know you are long gone. But I still wish I could remember why I did it for the first time, just to make sure you never come back ever again. Please don't come back again.

Interview with Parvinder

Tell me about each of your pieces Parvinder, and why you wrote them.

Firstly, I want to say that to me, any piece of paper is a room full of soft yellow flowers, sky-high mountains and a lush green oasis. Mum says I have always had a piece of paper in one hand and a pen in another. I am 20 years-old and I have seen very little of this world; I have read very little, learned very little. All these little bits have helped me to come up with the pieces that I have submitted for this book. Every piece that I submit to the universe has its strings attached to me. I wish reading this will help the readers to figure out how they have been feeling, because whenever I am able to give words or colours, or find sounds to my fears, they become a beautiful motion picture of the past and I am finally able to move away from it.

RED is a result of many different poems from when I was still younger with anger issues that were nothing like the ones that I now walk with. We all have a past coloured in the colour that we might not like and love at the same time. Mine is of the colour red. At some point, I realized that anger caused destruction and that I was hurting the ones that had nothing to do with the way that I was feeling. I knew I couldn't hurt them and I had recently heard of an alternative. Self-harm. As stupid as it sounds, it was deeply satisfying. From "oh let's just try it" I went to "huh I feel so happy, let's do it again". It was by far my stupidest decision. It is like smoking or any other addiction for that matter-of-fact. Once you are into it, only strong determination will help you get out. Once I knew it was wrong, thanks to the moon, I started looking for alternatives. I started painting, drawing, gardening, journaling. In other words, doing anything but that. It helped! Go for a jog, take boxing lessons, go for a walk; all of it helps! Take my word on it, the world is so much prettier outside Red.

It is true that we need to feel strongly to come up with something that holds the ability to move someone else. I'm not easily satisfied with what I write, but there are some pieces by the end of which I am ready to cry for a few good minutes. RED was one of them.

COMMENCING is very specifically about feeling numb. There were times when I found it so hard to feel anything at all. I didn't really cry when my Grandfather passed away. Not like I was super close to him, but he still was my Grandfather right? I was supposed to cry right?

But I couldn't. It bothered me so much. Just because everyone else was crying and I wasn't, I decided something was wrong with me. Only recently have I realized that it is okay to not be able to feel anything at all. Some of us are just made that way and that is okay. This is just an example, but there were always random instances when everyone else was crying and I wasn't; dreaded those moments. All I am saying is poking a blade through you is not a solution. Feeling pain this way is not a solution. Talk to anyone. Write it out. Go see a doctor whenever you think you need to, okay?! There are chemicals that your body needs to be happy, hormones and stuff I don't really know what they are but I know we need it. Be open about your struggles, if not because you need the help, then do it because someone else might!

BLADES is an angry piece. Sometime you just can't wait for it all to be over right. This was from then. I'm so glad I don't feel that way again. I keep myself so busy and I keep finding new things to do every day. Thus giving me a new reason to live every day.

REPETITION too is an angry one. I wish I could remember why I wrote it or what was the context. It never came back to me and it is a pretty old piece but I guess this happens to everyone. You know something in a moment and in the next, you forget if you were supposed to breathe out next or breathe in. I really hope this makes sense.

SCARS is a special one. You know those time when you just wish you could go back to those simple relations that you had with someone in your past? Maybe a friend or maybe just someone you nodded to in the hallway every day without fail. I hope we all have someone like that. Because when everyone else leaves, a smile from this person is enough for you to wake up with the next Sun. I try to be nice to everyone and people are nice and sweet back to me. I really wish we all would flash our wide smiles more often. I instantly want to be friends with anyone who is not shy to smile a big wide smile.

GENDERFLUID, a group of people not many talk about and I am not quite sure how to explain it myself. I know I am gender fluid for sure but I don't know how to explain it. And hence I don't have much to say about it, except that I am your sister and anyone who reads this is welcome to talk to me about anything at all.

The first drafts to most of these pieces were written in the shower. Yes, it is the best place for thoughts. And food courts, I love writing in food courts and cafes. So many people and so many emotion and food and coffee. All the amazing things.

To everyone reading this, I wish I could stress enough on the need to feel. Najwa Zebain said something I can never forget. She said; *'when pain knocks on your door, let it in. if you don't, it will knock harder. Its voice will become, louder and louder. So let it in. spend some time with it. Understand it. Then walk it to the door and tell it to leave because it's time for you to welcome happiness.'* I live by this poem. We need to honour pain, we need to understand it, but we also need to respect ourselves and know what is best for ourselves. Get hurt but heal. I hope all of us can heal.

Happy healing!

Read Parvinder's other pieces on pages 60, 95, 127, 146 and 151.

JIGSAW

By Nurah Harun.

The older I grow, the more I know,
Display of strength is a farce,
For long, I've hidden behind scars,
I've looked alright, had twinkle in my eyes,
But I've also cried all night.
I hide away, disallow my brokenness from display,
I wear make up, I suit up and walk upright,
And everyday I wonder, if I'll make it tonight?
I do pray to be okay, someday,
For now, self-destruction is my only way.
You wonder what I get, or whether I regret,
Hurting myself the way I do,
Self-harm is a vicious cycle of an emotional fool,
I want to stop, but I cannot,
Because I am far down the destructive path.
If you want to save me, you have to let me be,
But also hold me tight occasionally,
In my head everything is worse than the reality,
Everyday I write a song, from the broken parts of who I am,
Like I am a jigsaw puzzle that I'm trying to solve.

May be there is a way to be okay, but who's to say?
Unlike others, I find little of life to celebrate,
And for me, I wonder whether it's too late,
As life heckles, I subtly struggle - to choose life over knife, every other night,
Like sleep and death are the two sides of the same coin.

BEYOND THE POINT OF NO RETURN

By Nilanjana Bose

I. From the other side

A pearl button from my shirt fell
without my knowing, into a gale
and was swept along till it reached hell -
did you know hell was this cold?
There is no music, story, rhyme,
no epic verse, no lofty line
that can make torment feel sublime,
however sung or told.

Did I love too much or not enough,
and should there be cut offs for love -
so that it's not fully used up?
Couldn't find the replies.
Oh, everywhere I looked for you,
through screes and tracks, the earth's own swoosh
till there was nothing left to do
but stop and shut my eyes.

But I didn't mean to get so deep,
didn't mean to take that last trip,
I didn't mean to go to sleep,
let go of helping hands.
But I was tired - of this mess,
the black holes in an empty face,
the wings of wheeling nothingness -
I hope they'll understand.

II. From this side

Where have you gone, my dearest one
in which twisted valleys of pain?
The scree is sharp and no streams run -
why do you go that way?
I call and call, hold out my arms,
leave my doors wide, keep your rooms warm;
you never listen, nor turn and come,
you brush my love away.

Why have you gone, my dearest one,

on whip-thin paths, so hard to turn?
You're just a speck on the horizon -
why do you go so far
under callous skies, smoke and stone,
mushrooming clouds, tracks overgrown?
But know that you're never alone
- this heart's always ajar.

What have you done, my dearest one?
Come back from those caves of ruin,
from whirlpools of pain out in the sun,
come back, and let me help.
But you walk deeper, smaller, opaque
over the scree; the sharp-edged rock
splinters as you cascade and break.
And I shatter, myself.

I CAN REMEMBER HEAVEN

By Linda M. Crate

I will fight
the beasts inside of me
because I know
that life may not always be sweet,
but it need not be bitter;
I have known joy as deep as this pain
and so I will use every sunset
I can to burn away
every winter fang;
I am both life and death wrapped together
both dreams and nightmares,
but that doesn't mean I must die to all
the ugly things inside me—
I will always remember
that it is darkest before the dawn,
but without night there could be no beautiful
days;
and so I will be brave
even on the days where I feel weak and ugly
I will put one foot in front of the other
march forward no matter how slow
because progress is progress
no matter the speed—
sometimes I feel like I am alone
that no one hears me or loves me or cares,
but I look back at all the gifts I was given;
and photos help me remember
good times
I think that's why I take so many
so on the days where hell has come to me
I can remember heaven.

Interview with Linda

Why did you write your contributions Linda?

I wrote these poems because I want to be able to help people. They say to turn your pain into art, and I think that is good advice. It gives you the power over the situation, and helps you gain some insights into who you once were and what you were thinking. Once you're at that point you get to choose to move on in whatever way you can or change learned behaviour that may not be healthy or normal.

Were they based on personal experiences?

Yes. My uncle did take his own life when I was a teenager. It was heartbreaking. I really didn't realize he was struggling so badly. I was wrapped up in my own struggles and really wounded, and it made me sad that maybe on some level I pushed him away. I blamed myself for a long time. I thought maybe if he knew that I loved him or if I had made it a point to show him how much I loved him that he wouldn't have taken his own life.

Describe a little about how you felt at that time?

At the time when my depression was the strongest, I was a teenager. I was heavily bullied because I was shy, I refused to drink underage, I was a good girl and I was fat; anything you can think of people mocked me for. I began to think of myself as disposable and worthless. I began to see myself as a burden to everyone I loved. I was very critical of myself and that, combined with the bullying and arguments I sometimes had in my home life, created a very toxic environment for me. I managed to handle the situation by becoming comfortable with being alone. I realized that some people are bad for my health, and sometimes being alone is better than being around someone if they're going to make me feel bad about myself or treat me poorly. I also decided that I wasn't going to give the people the satisfaction of *getting* to me. That I was going to live my life to prove them wrong, to show them that I was a lot stronger and more capable than any of them gave me credit for. I told myself that I was going to get through this because high school wasn't forever.

Do you still suffer from depression?

Yes, I still suffer from bouts of depression but I take it a day at a time. Some days are easier than others. There are periods of time where I am completely fine, and there are others where I find myself having a bad mental health day and I try to use music or my writing to heal. To get all the ugly stuff out. I also try to remind myself of good times in life - I think that's why I like to take so many pictures with family and friends, so I have something good to hold onto. I hold onto old cards, too, to remind myself that there are people that do care about me. I also have my uncle's last letter to me, and I read it from time to time when I'm feeling down. He told me to pursue my dreams relentlessly, and that is what I hope to do. I hope one day I'll make him proud. I miss him very much. But his death taught me that I didn't want to die, I just didn't want to feel this way. So I try to choose happiness every day. Some days I am more successful at this than others.

What would you say to anyone going through similar emotions and experiences that you went through?

The advice I give anyone who is struggling is seek help is that it is okay to find someone who understands, and speak to them. Anyone who mocks you or is condescending about your mental health clearly hasn't understood what it is to struggle with your battle. Don't waste your time or energy with those sorts of people; they will always find a way to devalue you and your experiences. Find a way to express yourself, too, whether it's through dance, writing, music, sports, video games - whatever makes your heart happy. Find something to help you through because, in the end, we all have to save ourselves. People can help you through the struggle, but they *cannot* take the struggle away for you. Also if you have medications to deal with your depression then *please, please* take them. My uncle stopped taking them because he'd feel better, and then he'd spiral down into depression again. If you feel better, that's great, but please *keep* taking your medication so you can continue to feel better. Also, if your medication isn't working for you then try something else. Sometimes I've found being in nature helps me. Just being near the water or the trees is beneficial to my health, and I think we all need some fresh air every once in a while. And *VERY* important; remind yourself that you have a value and a worth, even if other people cannot always see it, and that you are loved more than you know. People aren't always going to reach out to you when you're struggling because some of them might not even notice, but that doesn't mean that they don't care. Sometimes we're all struggling through things of our own. Just be gentle with others and be gentle with yourself. Practice self-care; need a nap? Take one. Take a shower. Eat a piece of chocolate if that will make you feel better. Just take one day at a time, and try to breathe as best as you can. Not every day is going to be a good day, but there is something good to be found in each day even if it's something small. Try to retrain your brain to see the positives (no matter how small they may be), and find joy in simple things. It *really, really* makes a difference.

Read Linda's other pieces on pages 85, 120, 139, 149 and 168.

A FALLEN GRADUATE

By Donna Zephrine

There are some people who leave an impression in your mind even from just small conversations. They can impact a community without even knowing it.

Graduation day, May 17, 2017 all of the graduates assembled together at the Beacon Theatre ready to walk across the stage. I noticed a student with a bright gold medallion around his neck. He was the only one wearing it so I went up to him and asked what it symbolized. He stated he had not only received his master's in social work but also a minor in law. I was so impressed by not only his accomplishments but his clear popularity among the class and staff. He seemed so well-liked, so accomplished, and had a zest for life that was clear from just observing him.

Just about two weeks later, we received an email notifying our community that Stephen had passed away. He had taken his life. It was a tragic loss to his family and our Columbia family. I was in shock. I never would have thought Stephen would take his life. The email notifying us of his death also told us a little more about his wonderful life. I learned he was the editor of the Columbia University Social work Review magazine. He started an initiative during his master's to help those who were incarcerated to re-integrate into their families. Prior to his education at Columbia he served as a marine veteran oversees. In his spare time he was a DJ bringing happiness and music to others.

After learning so much about his life, I was even more shocked to know he took his life. He seemed to have it all. I was especially touched to learn of his veteran status as I too am a veteran. I wished I had known that sooner and that we could have bonded over our invisible wounds left by war. Many of us veterans have a soundtrack of war playing in our heads that never leaves us or lets us forget our experiences. It impacts everything we do. I wondered if he suffered from PTSD or if his war experienced contributed to his pain.

I wish I would have been able to have more conversations with him and get to know him more. The school held a memorial for him where students and his family members could speak of and celebrate his life. I unfortunately could not attend but received the memorial slide show to learn more about him. I realized from his photos that when I spoke to him at graduation I hadn't recognized that he was the same student I had passed by in the hallway or library. He had grown out a beard and was wearing sunglasses.

The school gave us his mother's contact information and I offered her my condolences and spoke of our shared veteran experience. I cannot imagine the loss she felt or the struggles his family went through.

I learned you never truly know what a person is going through. We are surrounded by people all the time, in all different settings and you never know what those people are carrying on their shoulders. Many who suffer from depression or suicidal ideas never tell anyone or let it show. Even those who seem to have the most going for them can be suffering and struggling inside. They may never know the impact they had on those they left behind.

FOR PAUL

By Chrys Salt

'*And now one final dive*
into a dry pool,' you wrote.
Your suicide note
left on the table by an empty cup –
before your reckless arrow of descent
sped headlong to the crags below
the gorge with all the rash abandonment
of youth that could not know
or count the cost to those alive

and did not, in that moment,
care.

How could imagination dare
your poised intent
that fatal plummet down the cliff
the crush of skull on rock
the after-shock of rage and grief –

so we freeze-frame you in mid-air
because we must -
an arc of flight against the cumulus
with all our hopes for you
suspended there.

WALLS

By Bill Cox

Be a man
I was told,
Build a wall.
Make it high,
Make it strong,
So no-one
Can ever
Get in.
I sat behind
My wall looking
Out at the world.
My pain had
Nowhere to go.
I could not
Connect
Because of
My wall.
I felt anger
Fear
Sadness
But no one
Could hear
My Cry
Because of
My Wall.
So I punched
And punched
Until the wall
Crumbled.
With bloody hands
I reached out
Until I felt
The joy
The necessity
Of human connection.
Now I teach
My son,
Be a man son,
Do not hide,
But stand
And face the world

Hand in hand
With the people
By your side.

Interview with Bill

Tell me about the circumstances behind your pieces Bill?

Harry's suicide happened when I was in the army, during the mid-1990s. We'd been in the same platoon during our previous posting in Berlin, and had gotten quite friendly – I remember going out on the town on the last night of our tour there and a group of us, including Harry, staggering back home along the wide Berlin avenue's signing *Flower of Scotland* at the top of our voices.

When the Regiment moved to Northern Ireland we ended up in different platoons, though we would still have a chat whenever our paths crossed. Halfway through our tour there something happened to Harry that sent him off the rails. He signed a couple of pistols out of the armoury and ran amok for a few hours, taking pot-shots at buildings, but without any apparent desire to harm others.

We were all confined to Barracks, but the final scenes played out on the parade square, which all the accommodation blocks looked onto. Harry, followed at a respectful distance by the camp guard (who had orders to shoot him if he presented an imminent threat to anyone) ended up on the helipad on the parade square.

In full view of his fellow soldiers he had a last shouted conversation with the base 2IC before he put a pistol to the side of his head and pulled the trigger. He was dead before he hit the ground.

We never did find out the reason behind Harry's rampage and suicide, what factors drove him amok. There were rumours about a broken relationship with his girlfriend, but nothing was ever substantiated. It seems clear though that some form of stress drove him over the edge.

Watching the incident was both shocking and unreal. I'd liked Harry; we'd been friends, but it was perhaps the unreality of the situation that was the greater emotion. What had happened was so bizarre, so unexpected – Harry was generally quite a mild-mannered character and had seemed happy in a quiet and reserved way.

Because the whole episode had been so public (it was in the national press the next day) there was almost a collective response to it. The CO gathered the Regiment the next day and I remember him saying that we should remember the Harry of better times; "*not the monster we saw last night"*. I wonder now at that remark, because it downplays the episode in a way. If it was the work of a 'monster' then we don't have to examine it in any detail.

However, if we think of that episode as the act of a man who was suffering, perhaps in response to stress or emotional distress, then it can be seen as preventable. It is also something that could happen to anybody.

When I was younger I perhaps saw suicide as a sign of mental weakness or instability. However, as I have experienced more in my life, I've come to appreciate how fragile our minds are, how sometimes we can lose control of our emotions, our confidence and self-worth. Again, in my youth I always believed in the myth of the true man as a lone wolf, that true masculinity meant not needing anybody else.

However, I now see that that idea is a fallacy, a vision propagated by an idealised macho culture that is toxic to true masculinity. All of us need the company and companionship of others. We are a social species and isolation is the worst thing you can do to a social animal.

Harry obviously felt a great deal of emotion, whether anger, sadness or despair before he took his own life. If he had been able to share that burden through talking then perhaps his death could have been averted.

Read Bill's other pieces on pages 119, 145, 170.

A HEADS-UP DREAM FOR PEACE

By Mark Blickley

I resent when beheading videos go viral and zombie apocalypses top viewer entertainment lists as it makes it much too easy for them to ignore the walking dead sharing a subway ride on way to a final destination that proves being heads-up simply exposes one as too easy a target regardless of the helmet I first wear in boot camp when angry drill sergeants scream at me during squadron manoeuvrers to pull my head out of my ass so I don't kill my buddies because of a lack of concentration though I was concentrating real hard when Happy Jack took the two shots to the head that exploded his Chicago style ghetto humour all over my face and flak jacket dripping down inside sand coated combat boots that allow me to walk away and proclaim heads you lose but tales you win if you're alive and able to speak of them to a passenger audience who bury their heads in smart phone images and sounds to avoid their neighbour's headless pain of surrender seated alone across the aisle where no one else sits to coax a face from my torn and stained civilian clothes while the train chugs to the South Ferry final stop where a whiff of rusty river replaces my body odour and signals a free boat ride that promises freedom when midway to Staten Island it glides past the Statue of Liberty and I plunge towards the crowned Lady who will read my DD214 safely wrapped in protective plastic and pinned to my pants pocket along with instructing letter that will guide me towards my very own plot of land in lovely Virginia where I can sleep with silent brothers and sisters and share a peace my grateful government will mark and preserve with a uniformly crafted and informative headstone...

Excerpted from the 2019 text based art book collaboration *Dream Streams,* with fine arts photographer Amy Bassin.

LETTERS

By Ebuwa Ohenhen

Dear shrink,
They have returned,
Those demons I told you about
Demons that look exactly like me
Can you fix me?

Dear Father,
I'm possessed
Would you perform an exorcism?
But how do you cast out the devil
From himself?

Dear Father,
Your son is saying goodbye,
This world was always a vacation
And my life was always an illusion.

Dear mother,
Your sun is saying goodbye
I'm sorry for all the lies
You are the sweetest thing
since dodo and beans.

Dear bestie,
This is goodbye,
Sorry for the hurts I caused
Sorry for the pain I'm about to cause

Dear God,
your son is coming home.
Your son is dead.

THE LAST GOODBYE

By Bee Parkinson-Cameron

Dear Father,

> I always questioned why you didn't support me,
> In any of my endeavours?
> You were always selective
> And I never met the grade.

I used to try so hard
To be a daughter
That you could be proud of,
That you could be proud to call your own.

> But the strain of the lie was too much
> I denied myself for you
> And I couldn't keep doing it,
> I couldn't maintain the pretence.

I gave up. I tried to change myself
I tried to unashamedly be the real me.
You recoiled in disgust,
When I held out my hand to you.

> You couldn't love me when I tried
> To be who I thought you wanted
> Me to be.
> I was never that person.

I tried to be myself for you
That was never enough either
So why bother anymore?
Why bother with any of it?

> You will never support or love me
> I accept that I failed to be your Princess
> I accept that I failed from my first breath.

This is the last goodbye
To you
To the world
To me.

> Yours, Brooke

Interview with Bee

How does poetry help you emotionally Bee?

For me, my poetry and by extension the rest of my writing has been my way of making sense of the world around me and some of my own experiences. For every piece that I write, a small piece of my soul spills out onto the page.

What was the first piece you wrote and why?

The first real poem I ever wrote was a piece called *Dove*, which many people believed to be quite a beautiful piece. However, to me, *Dove* was my first suicide note; the only part of me that I was going to leave behind. If I was going to die, I wanted to leave behind something beautiful as my mark upon the world.

How did your mental and emotional health deteriorate?

I have experienced many traumas in my life and these have taken their toll on me. Self-harming was a way of coping when I felt like I was breaking at the seams. It wasn't a good way of coping, by any stretch of the imagination, but at the time it felt like it was the only thing I had. It became an addiction actually, my way of surviving in an unforgiving world. When I cut myself, I watched the blood sliding down my skin and, for those few moments, I felt as though all the pain that was in my heart was being released. It was the ultimate catharsis. It took me years and a lot of healing to understand that it wasn't actually helping me, I just thought that it was.

In 2012, I managed to escape an abusive relationship, but my mental health was very fragile. I suppose, in a way, it was almost inevitable that I would find myself at rock bottom. In 2013, I took an overdose. To my shame, I swallowed approx. 50 pills, one after the other, in front of my friend while we were talking on Skype. It had been unforgivable and callous of me. I had thought nothing of his feelings, only my own pain. If it hadn't been for him, no one would have called the ambulance and I might not be here now. One of the paramedics who picked me up admonished me heavily. She was very angry with me for being stupid and she let that anger show. She had no idea what I had been through, to her all she probably saw was wasted potential, another young person trying to throw their life away.

How did you feel in the hospital?

I felt so lonely sitting in the hospital bed. The nurse asked me if I wanted them to call my parents and I said no, I didn't. I felt shame and confusion. I had made the decision that I didn't want to be there anymore and that I couldn't stand all of the feelings that were inside of me. I had thought I had been in love and that had been taken from me; the trust I placed in another human being had been twisted and distorted and I had lost my innocence. I had always believed in the good in people, but I had been proven wrong... or so I thought.

After some time had passed and the fear of my father's anger had abated, I realised that there were only three people I wanted with me; my parents and my best friend who had saved my life. I relented and I quietly whispered to the nurse that I wanted my parents to know where I was.

And what did your parents think?

My parents were angry, but it was a different kind of anger; I can only imagine how they must have felt, finding out the dirty details of their only daughter's suffering. Were they upset that I hadn't come to them? Probably. Since that day, I have never kept any of my pain secret from my parents. I have let them support me through the difficult parts of my life and now, I have a loving husband who does the same for me and encourages me when I feel like I am failing to swim against the tide of emotions and thoughts, the inky darkness of the sea threatening to drown me.

Was this the first time you thought about taking your own life?

No, my journey between thinking of suicide and attempting to commit it was a long one. The first time I wanted to die I was eight years old. I remember distinctly sitting in the girl's toilets, hiding from my bullies, feet curled up on the toilet seat so they didn't know I was in the stall. I thought about the world I was living in, I thought about my place, my insignificance in the grand scheme of things and I thought to myself that no one would miss me when I was gone. Make no mistake, I had a loving family and I still do. The problem is that darkness in me, that constant fight to remain in the light when all the misery and depression and the monstrous shapes in the shadows leered at me. I was young, I should never have been in the position where I wanted to die.

I was twenty when I swallowed those pills. I overdosed on a combination of citalopram and ibuprofen and, to this day, I cannot take either of those medications. I try to take ibuprofen for muscular pain and my throat closes up, my body refuses to let me swallow the pill. I will tell you this now, the stomach pain that I experienced in the days following my overdose were awful. I would wake up in my bed, clutching my stomach, crying and screaming with the physical pain. I felt as though I was being ripped apart, physically and emotionally.

How did your overdose affect you emotionally?

The overdose signalled a large turning point in my life and, in a perverse sort of way, was one of the best things to happen to me. Let me explain: When you have fallen so far, when your arse has hit rock bottom, you look around and take stock and you realise that there's only place for you to go. You can't fall any further than you already have and so you know that whatever comes next, you can make it through. At least, that's how it seemed to me. I finally received the proper medical treatment that I should have received all those years previously. An emotionally unstable personality disorder, that was the answer. I had a genetic predisposition towards it, but all the trauma in my life had been the catalyst for its development. The bullying, the steady destruction of my sense of self confidence and self-worth by my male love interests (some worse than others), the abuse and the loss of my beloved grandpa to terminal cancer that slowly devoured him in front of me (even beginning to change who he was as a person) among other things, had proved too much for my mind to handle. There was no weakness in that though and the break was clean and because of that, I have been able to heal.

Make no mistake, I still experience issues with my condition, but the medication regime that I have, and the support from my doctor, has been life changing. My quality of life now is something that, when I was sitting in that hospital bed, I could only have dreamt of. I have taken all the trauma of my life and I have stood up to it; faced the demons of my past (most of them), and I have not let them define me or my future. I have grown and gone from strength to strength over the years, and now I mostly have things under control. Sometimes I still think about suicide, but I do it now more with a sense of curiosity and with the drive to raise awareness of the issue in the hope that I can help save even just one person from themselves. We need to make our voices loud and clear; to let people know that everything they are feeling is okay but that ending it all, snuffing out their beautiful and wonderful life is not the answer. The pain feels all encompassing; it feels as though it is robbing your breath and that you will die anyway but please, listen to me and hold on. Just you keep holding on and someone will be there to take your hand and give you the strength you need to climb back from the edge.

And where are you now, emotionally?

It has been nearly seven years since my overdose and in that time, I have found real love, I have made a home for myself with my husband, I have forged new friendships and rekindled old ones. I have learned so much about the world around me, I have been published in several anthologies, and I have created and produced two stage plays, one of which covers my own experiences of domestic abuse and has brought solace and comfort to other survivors.

I will always be that woman in the hospital bed, but I am also the successful woman I am now. Like the phoenix, I rose from the ashes and I am glorious. To anyone else reading this who is struggling; you *can* do this, I know you can do this, and you too are glorious, if only you will stop being so hard on yourself and embrace your inner beauty. Reach out to your friends and family, no matter how much your brain screams at you that they don't care, I can assure you that they do. Don't struggle in silence, speak, and find your own freedom from that.

From beautiful poetry now to crassness, my final words can be summarised as follows; fuck everyone and everything who drags you down and you fly high you magnificent being.

Read Bee's other pieces on pages 77, 113 and 126.

THE AFTERMATH

By Ibn Qalam

I thought 'that' would be it, when eventually the end came,
Processed and prodded, photographed and listed.
The confusing mix of relief and blame,
And gradual dawnings with priorities shifted.

Outside the wind blew and the sun shone,
As season's greetings spray painted reality.
Smiles, tears and drinks for everyone,
Veneered the injustice and shame and formality.

The prayers answered, according to some,
And Gods intervention to make our lives whole,
In ignorance of the torture and how I'd succumb,
To his will, kindness and preordained role.

The fug rests cloudy, cartoon-like but real,
Overhead in threat of drizzle or Donner and Blitzen,
Always reminding me that risking the act to feel,
Is fraught with danger, peril, risk but unwritten.

The energy that's blessed, and cursed, me all my life
Has vanished, as has the nervous vigour that sustained it.
Smiling and humble whilst gracious and safe,
Sapped totally, secretively, lest any proclaim it.

Carry me and give me cash, take that burden away
Enlist all the charities, phone all the millionaires,
Deposit or exchange the cheer and joy of the day,
Or don't I stand a sodding prayer?

Too hot to employ, too weary to care,
The future's uncertain, predictably so,
I've got to be rid of the bloody affair
And reap the advice I too often bestow.

Interview with Ibn

Tell me about your thoughts behind your poems Ibn?

Writing is a way of committing thoughts to a place and period in time. The page listens and never judges. It asks just that you'll find the courage to subtly allude to your innermost thoughts in as abstract a way as you like. Your emotions may be hidden in the open with readers, imagined or real, each taking a piece of your perceived burden each time they read. It's sharing, but not sharing, because every individual will take a unique meaning away with them. If asked *"When you said this what did you mean"*, it's incumbent upon the author to say *"Whatever you see or understand must be the meaning."* In trying to comprehend one's own emotions, commitment to writing can add form and structure to a difficult experience that may, in itself, be formless and chaotic. I find comfort in order.

How were you feeling at the time of writing?

I imagine I was feeling helpless. When 'big things' happen in one's life, I mean, life changing events that are out of your control and that seem to take on a life of their own to which you must simply react because you have no influence, your status has been compromised and downgraded, you rely on paid strangers to represent you and no one you know is willing to get too involved. Your savings very quickly evaporate and associates and fair-weather friends stop taking or returning your calls. One's ability to manage is immediately sorely tested, and your shortcomings or, less tolerant character facets are exaggerated, to your eternal shame. The black cloud hovers. Immovably. Gatherings meant to celebrate have the opposite effect and the cracks in one's public persona become gorges. You retreat, stunned by life, shocked by your own inability to deal with people who don't see the depths of the damage, who'll continue to demand of you, unaware that you are far from able of delivering anything. In this condition, with this condition the love of your closest partner becomes a matter of life and death.

Were these feeling over something specific or a specific event?

Yes, the 'event' that dominated my life for 10 years officially ended in December 2018. Over that period of time I lived in a state of constant fear. Not just for myself but for those that I loved and those than relied on me. I went from able, assured, confident, productive, humorous and popular to withdrawn, overweight, dark, aggressive, self-medicated, hyper-cynical, distrusting and pessimistic. For nearly five of those years I 'numbed out' on anti-depressants which had a terrifying effect when coupled with heavy drinking, which added nightmarishly to the fear and gave me palpitations every day. Sleep was rarely pleasant, so fitful and surreal unconsciousness became its replacement. Compared to the normality of everyday life, the stark concurrence of emotions made the dark much much darker.

How was this resolved?

I have alluded to 'The event' and won't share details of what it was, but I will share the emotional devastation wrought by it. The resolution came about through the intervention of people of conscience who recognized my spiritual and emotional degradation after my partner and closest allies presented the facts to them. By now I had become so incapable and inept at presenting myself as anything but useless and appalling, that their kind and selfless support kept my head above water long enough for the septic tank to be drained and I could once more stand, albeit on shaky legs at the bottom of a tank!

How did you move past this challenging time?

I haven't really. You don't just 'move past' it. But you do learn to live with it. The knowledge I mean. You begin to accept was has happened and you stop punishing yourself for events that are in the past and unchangeable. Can't change the past, right? So stop fretting about that which has occurred and now cannot be altered.

I fell into literature, entirely. I read and read and read. I tried to find answers to the human condition - not my condition you understand - the whole human condition. Why do people do and say the things they do and say? Lofty ambitions, but also deeply comforting. Knowing that minds from the past had experienced similar to me was a revelation. It also felt like I was somehow strengthening my core, my mind was at least absorbing wisdom which was a respite from the self flagellation of tearful 4am black dog.

Everybody is aware of *"To be or not to be"* from Hamlet, but few continue the soliloquy which is a shame because it's utterly brilliant

> *"To be, or not to be, that is the Question:*
> *Whether 'tis Nobler in the mind to suffer*
> *The Slings and Arrows of outragious Fortune,*

Or to take Armes against a Sea of troubles,
And by opposing end them:"

"*And by opposing end them*", I took to heart.

How do you feel now?

I'm OK Thanks. Time helps. It's darkest before the dawn etc., I'm mending. I tried to revive my empathy for others and in helping them, help myself. Is any act entirely selfless? I don't know; some maybe. I have tried to understand the difference between justifiable anger and destructive anger. In doing so I've avoided self-righteous indignation at 'what they did to me' and consigned the episode to 'Bad people will do bad things and good people will do good things…surround yourself with good people.' My confidence is still being rather bashful but I'll strong-arm him out into the open soon enough for a one man show I want to call *Schizophrenia*. Performing in front of an audience is like bungee jumping every minute. It is totally terrifying but essential therapy in taking arms against a sea of troubles and in opposing end them.

I'm not pursuing happiness, but I do want to be content. That'll do.

Do you have any advice for anyone else going through similar emotions?

Keep at it.
Dig deep.
Be charitable.
Be kind.
Talk always. Find your confidant/s and keep talking. Bore them to pieces, it doesn't matter they're there to listen.
Build your empathy for others.
Don't sweat the small shit.
Face your accusers. Face your fear.
Walk. Swim.
Eat well. Red meat sometimes. Veggies always.
Get a pet.
Sing loudly and badly for as long as you can.
Learn three chords on a guitar or piano, you'll be able to play hundreds of songs. Cry. Don't hold it in or try to dismiss it, you'll feel better afterwards. Learn *Desiderata* off by heart. "*With all its sham, drudgery and broken dreams, it is still a beautiful world.*"

Read Ibn's other pieces on pages 147, 184.

PAIN AND GRIEF

By Richard Goss

As I see you
lying there,
in pain and in grief,
I know why you did what you did,
to attempt suicide,
I know you want to be free of pain,
and grief,
but you can't,
not yet,
because you are a dad,
and a grandad,
and you have a family who cares.
Please, please talk to me.

OFF THE SIDE

By Pamela Scott

Stop,
centre of
the bridge. Breathe.

Stare
out at
the water. Contemplating.

Grief
like a
small angry child.

Grief
kicks my
ribs. Always screaming.

Grief
hisses, spits
like someone mad.

How
easy, to
climb up, over.

Spread
arms, leap
into your darkness.

Fall
Forever, never
hit the ground.

How
pointless and
easy death is.

Grief
makes everything
hurt. New aches.

Rage
makes me
unable to speak.

How
dare you
leave me here.

SAUDADE

By Hannah Louise MacFarlane

"a deep emotional state of nostalgic or profound melancholic longing for an absent something or someone that one loves"

I miss her on a Monday when the week is new and there is a whole life to be had. When from the dream catcher filled paradise that I hope she presides in catches all of my nightmares and I sleep through the night. When I have questions and she's not there to answer them. It's like missing a silhouette of a person you may have known but never got the chance to, because I never got to know her as well as I got to know the trauma that she left behind.

I don't blame her on a Tuesday when I wake up sad and unable to leave my bed. I don't blame her for the sadness that lives on both of my shoulders and pushes me deep into the quicksand. I don't even blame her for my complex understanding of how cruel the world is, depicted in my journals from age ten. I don't blame her for wanting to leave, I don't blame her for the fact that she did, but sometimes, on a Wednesday, I wish that I did.

I want to get to know her on a Thursday. I sit with old pictures and laugh at hairstyles and my tongue burns from wanting to know what made her so sad. I look for answers at the bottom of boxes and never ask the questions that run riot in my mind but never reach a voiced existence because not everyone is as blame free Tuesday as I am, and I have grown to understand why. Actions have consequences and our entire existence was turned into a consequence the second she died.

I think about her all day on a Friday. When I step on the train to get to class on time, and when the tannoy reads the name of the station I wince in my seat and hold back tears because I have never fully understood. When I get off the train at my destination and those fourteen minutes last fourteen years I think back ten and imagine how different life would be now; then paint on my best smile when someone asks what's wrong.

I forget about it all on a Saturday because it's my self-proclaimed day off from the things that make me sad. Although the list is long and plentiful I put it to one side and think about the future that I have and have yet to know I have. I try and not worry about the past because living there part time has been exhausting and I'm desperately trying to cut down on the commute.

I wallow in it on a Sunday. When I am tired and preparing for the week ahead, when I catch a glimpse of the scars on my wrists that have faded but exist just enough for me to know that they are there. Metaphorically they live on my skin, a reminder of the horrors that have passed but not passed fast enough for me to miss them damaging my heart along the way. I wallow in her death and the death of happiness that existed for the years since she left-hand and left my mother with the weight of the world on her shoulders and her mother with her heart in her hands.

I learn from it every day. When everything inside pushed me to end my life I remembered the way it shaped my existence and the lessons I learned about life long before my time. I close my eyes and flashed before them are my niece who resembles me at that time; and then open them with a startle at the sadness that presides when I imagine a little boy growing up without me by his side. I will never do what has been done to me, because not only one person dies inside when someone commits suicide.

BLEED

By Bernadette Perez

Seep onto the pages of my life
Detach

Circulate
Run off the edge
Drip
Drain union of flood

Uncontrolled rapid release
Escape closed systems
Valves no longer clogged
Free flowing

Drown in knowledge
Access resources
Erase images from your chambers

Lost in process
Read between the lines

Treat text as illustration
Print copies as they are
Colour seeping dye adjacent
Vision apparent on brighter hues
Slowly I lose you

I am cut
Concern has opinion
Beyond space inconsistencies
I assure you I am conscious
Coherent not so
My thoughts dismantled
Drawn from artistry
Splattered

Empty pockets
Sunk into despair
Famished
Sucked dry
Bones brittle
I crumble

Liquid evaporates
Moisture diffused in small qualities
Spatters upon surface

Stabilize the air stream
Cut off at mainstream
Apply pressure
Stop the bleed
Stabilize

Stories jumbled
Continue to review
Read stained articles
Interpret its matter
Act quickly

As the grass is dead
Fertilizer seeps in
I soak into the soil
Grasping for life

Bounce back
Hail from dormancy
Rain continuously
Survive the shifting tempest

In my defense it was a miserable day

Speechless
I utter madness
Thy heart bleeds
An internal ache
Absolute chaos
I mourn the calm waters of a mill pond
Exhausted I bled dry

BLADES

By Parvinder Kaur

I try all its edges and press it against my curves.
And as soon as I lift it up again, I crave it back where it burns.

This flimsy stainless steel has now started to rust.
So I force the rust inside my wounds but it still doesn't burn enough.

I'm craving it on me again, I'm craving it so bad.
You have no idea when I talk about how I'm going mad.

My ink flows in different patterns, black on pages and red on curves.
I wonder how long until I run out of words.

SUICIDE NOTES: MINDSET

By Margareth Stewart

Oh grave,
graveyard, my best friend.
So cool and horny!
I'm so bullied and bored.
My tears so sorry and tempted.
You are my best friend - Gray.
Abused – Obtuse - Occludes
Trapped in a triangle. I am.
Tormented when my soul is in peace.
I must go. I knew it from the start.
From when I saw her quote years ago in San Francisco: *"From here I
depart, I hope never to come back."* I thought – *"fucking brave
woman."* Then, I grew up to be just like her.
It would be okay to come back if circumstances changed, but they
won't.
Why are people so sceptical? So, demanding?
There´s more ahead.
There's nothing reasonable in thinking rationally in a world whose
mind has lost itself in drugs, guns and pharmakos. Yes, pharmakos
will make my day.
I am making amends with the ground.
Stop the searching for reasons, motives, explanations.
There's none.
As simple as that.
It´s the world that has been messed up.
Chaotically and catastrophically - I'm not!
I'm crystal clear and blue.
It's not a matter of opinion, but evidence.
Compulsory evidence of a symptomatic world freaking with the ones
who go...
Sorry.
There are no doubts, no second thoughts - no minimum decoded
status of wanting to fail about it.
I'm a winner. I've planned it - a 3D business plan.
I took care of every single detail. Successful in all ventures.
To fail in such grand act would be fatal, not to say comical. A disaster
to both worlds.
No need to rush anything either.
The long and winding road will take us all there. Sooner or later -
while draining flesh's blood and sperm.
I am not down, I'm an enthusiast – stop the judgement and

condemning.

Moral values have joined us, too.

The fact is - it is getting too hot, climate change makes people want some refreshment, and it's cooler in here.

That's all.

Interview with Margareth

What motivated you to write this piece Margareth?

Oh, I wrote it inspired in many stories I've heard about suicide. People who wished to depart, others who could not do it, and I cannot ever forget Frida Kahlo who once wrote; *"from here, I depart happily and wish never to return."* So, it felt like I was hearing all these people asking the world not to crucify them, to stop judging them and let them die in peace. I just wrote what I've heard down, and that made this poem so unique.

Was it based in any personal experience?

No, I love living. But I know people who just wish to die, go, depart, leave, people who do not mind death at all. They are too many now, from teenagers to elderly; with motives or without motives, they simply did not enjoy life. The rise on suicidal rate all over the world does not allow us to forget that. It is alarming. Even though, there are major programs calling for actions and prevention, it is a hard target. On top of all that, more and more people are diagnosed with depression. There may be a link between depression and suicide, so once they are diagnosed with depression, medication is on the rise to prevent any sort of constraint. It seems like a very depressive never ending circle in a disrupted world... in which humanity does not know how to deal with it. To sum up, I would say suicide is a double death - the person who is already dead dies once more.

What did you base your piece on?

There has always been so much talk about suicide and the condemning of the 'dead' as if he or she was guilty or had no right to do so. I really wanted to the call attention to the fact that that could be a personal choice. So, my trigging emotion was being an empath to the dead. Being comprehensible enough to understand the reasons to commit it. I guess that is the originality of the poem, the point of view (POV). All the rest assumes that the author is being faithful to the voice of the dead. Instead of judging the victim, the poem is an attempt to solidarize with the dead. This change of point of view may bring new insight to this old problem.

Do you have any advice for someone going through depression or suicidal thoughts?

I'd ask them to reconsider, but unless there are more reasons to stay than to go, they may have second thoughts.

A TENDENCY TO OVERTHINK

By Barbara Hawthorn

I keep on breathing... in out...in out
Why? To carry on is unbelievable
Sixteen breaths per minute by my count
- Nine hundred and sixty in an hour –
Call it a thousand, an easy amount
If you want to calculate it further
... a day... heaven forbid, a year -
No, that's inconceivable
What a waste of oxygen that someone else could use.
And all the while like a well wound clock
My pulse beats on. That too must stop
Four beats per futile breath. I must call a halt
But how do I end it? What method to choose?
To turn off this engine and throw away the key?
An overdose? A drowning? Not too violent
Not too slow. Nothing too messy. That's not me.
Nothing too dramatic at the end of a rope
Just what do you do when you've lost all hope?
Where's pen and paper, let me make a list
Pedantic, I know, but what have I missed?
How can I die? *"Let me count the ways..."*
Oops... Oh no. That really is the end
I have gone and stolen Shakespeare's phrase!

TOO LATE

By Anonymous

I see you now
through a slit
in the wrist,
where the vein splits
into rapid droplets
to a white tile square.

I hear you
in the dripping,
in my breathing,
in the shock
spreading.

Your hand
is in this too.
Draining meaning,
making life and death
an otiose undertaking

SUICIDAL

By Nikori Ese Praise

Her eyes says something and her lips another.
She's hurt,
She's broken,
She's in pain
But she's hidden it in those eyes where you can't discover.
She's crying inside,
Her eyes show it but you're blinded by its glow.
Her eyes are speaking,
But you don't hear it.
The pain is right in her eyes, yet you don't see it.

She's saying something,
She's saying goodbye.

CHOICE

By Ebuwa Ohenhen

Root yourself in this moment,
Take a knee,
Breathe

Know that it is okay,
Not to be okay

Know that if you're
Strong enough to end it all,
Then you're also
Strong enough to fight it.

I need you,

Stay
For me

Fight
With me.

We will win.

SUICIDE

By Zahra Zuhair

Kiss my fingers
and hold me up.
Dance with my body
to the music of the wind, and
let me sway
gently with you underneath me.
Shut the noise
of the world out.
Give me your salty smell
and lull me to sleep
with the sweet music
of your breathing,
and when I have slept
swallow me whole
and take me
like a lover would take
my breath away.

Interview with Zahra

Why did you write this poem Zahra?

I was battling depression from dealing with a personal experience; a loss of sorts. In the process, I lost myself and if it wasn't for my family, my friends and my faith in God, I probably would not have come out of it. During the time, I contemplated suicide almost regularly, and often found myself alone in my room for hours lost in dark thoughts. This went on for a few months, which doesn't seem like much in a whole stretch of life, but can feel like eons to one experiencing it. And so I wrote this poem at a time when I had started mentally healing myself and the poem is one of acceptance to me.

Acceptance of what?

Acceptance that suicide will never be an option for me because it can never be because of my faith, an understanding of why this is significant to me in the larger scheme of things, and a hope that my life can offer to others what I cannot share in death. In accepting this, I found myself moving on from wishing death upon me – and one wishes death not for the sake of dying, but for the escape that it brings. I found comfort in teaching myself to manage suicidal thoughts by assigning them a dream like role in my mind. This forced me to accept that it can only be a dream and never a reality, much like the experience itself that I was recovering from. I would not say that this a solution for everyone, or that it was an easy thing to do, but it worked for me (not always but most times) and when one is mentally ready, it might work for them too.

Did you write it for yourself, or for someone else?

I wrote this poem for myself and I go back to it every now and then as though it were a portal to the dream I speak of, but I share it for others who are going through the same in this dark and murky world. Dealing with suicide brings many challenges, and only one of them is the battle one fights with or against oneself; only one of these challenges revolves around oneself. And this should not be the case for it a great battle. People around you can make it hard by judging you for being selfish, for not giving you enough space, for calling you weak but there is great selflessness in taking time to heal yourself before the world can have you, and there is great strength and courage in accepting your fate and allowing yourself to embrace and live your emotions, for this will allow you to face them, and to overcome them, you must face them. This also allows you to explore them, and from the exploration of your emotions, you discover yourself and perhaps your art, as is the case with me.

How do these thoughts of suicide and self-harm conflict with your culture?

In my culture, we do not talk about issues like this – depression, suicide and so on. Therefore, speaking about this openly is a big deal and done at the risk of scrutiny from, and gossip by, the members of my community. It is a sad fact that people tend to take for entertainment what should be empathized with or outcast what should not be suffered in silence. Being aware of this, I think it is important that some of us take it upon ourselves to be open about it in every way, even if it considered an act of rebellion, something unnecessary by those in our community. Here, I take that step. We need rebels for sure to make people realize that contemplating suicide isn't what makes you a rebel. It makes you human. Talking about it makes you a rebel, and there are great implications in such an act for our future.

LUCID LIE

By Pasithea Chan

Life or death are all in a moment
Defined as the beginning or the end.

Hurt is a moment that grows
narrowing your soul
in the back of your throat.

Joy is a moment that fades
running like a flash faster
than what your eyes catch.

We begin life in a moment
decided by two hearts in love.
We leave or end life in a moment
of sickness, mishap or disbelief.

No one can predict that moment
that begins or ends life.
Yet again no one can reason
with that moment, we just
accept it and move on.

Some think faith is a moment
of strength and light.
But I say to those that the dark
is a moment deeper and bigger
than light in impact and endurance.

Reason for an early end
are all in a moment
of pain beyond relief
of fear beyond safety
of loneliness beyond company
of guilt beyond forgiveness
of desertion beyond belonging
of distrust beyond trust.

You can live and choose your moment
You can describe, shape and colour your moment
but you can not describe others' moments.
For only the one whose skin holds

the blade within
is well versed and akin
with the pain caving in.

But again life is a moment
that takes a heart
to hold on to
for it is a hot coal
that scorches within
before it touches the skin.

I've been
taken by a moment
dark from within.
I've been to the land of despair
before where life could offer no more
but the truth is when you die everyday
the reason to end life early
ceases to be so canny.

An early exit is supposed
to bring relief or save what's left within.
What good is a save if there's nothing
left to save to begin with?
And so I say my life is a moment
of courage to accept the loss within
knowing there's nothing more to cave in.

You and I know it's all in a moment
and moments are always going by.
You can't stop time
by opting to die
such is a lucid lie.

Author notes: Inspired by Andy Black - *Put the Gun Down.*

116 123
By Hannah Louise MacFarlane

I know what you're thinking.
Nobody will notice if you're gone.

Every person has a life experience,
A cask of poison and mirth coating their existence; alluding itself in
an equilibrium we all hope to balance on like a pin prick between libra
and destruction.

Every person has a life expectancy,
Not rooted in the longevity of your pulse but the expectation of
success or failure rooted into your soul from the second you are born;
due to class, race, gender, and a multitude of pre requisite lists and
empty boxes you will either succumb to or disprove.

Every person has a life excitement,
A multitude of childhood ambition and hope for the future;
superheroes and firemen, astronauts and teachers, we are taught to
imagine the most exciting and theoretical possibilities for our wildest
dreams but so few of us manage to wrangle to tools to feel successful
or become a self diagnosed worthy person.

Every person has a choice,
Not born from expectation, experience or foreign excitement but born
from struggle and hardship. To carry the burden of the soul
wrenching despair you place upon your own hollowed shoulders or to
surrender to the pain and give up.

I know what you're thinking.
Nobody will notice if you're gone.

But you will,
You will notice as your life leaves your body or in the seconds before
you part from your soul that the strength it took to take your life was
misplaced; and redirecting that strength into fighting for yourself
would be worth it one day. That joy was yours as a birth right
because you don't have to be in a constant fight alone.

You are not alone.
People will notice if you're gone.

Those with a conscience like mine that watches statistics rise and people loose their lives.

You are not alone. You are a light within a world that burns brighter, lasts longer and flows harder than most; because the pain in your soul that has caused your grief is a credit to each day you survive. Your strength is unparalleled; but you don't have to carry the burden yourself.

There is someone waiting on the end of a phone line, desperate to help your heart heal towards the light that is within you. You are the sun. You are not your circumstance or situation; you are the sun, and you deserve to burn bright, not burn out.

Samaritans - 24 Hours - Call 116 123.

SHE DREAMS OF RIVERS

By Mike Rollins

Her skin
shines in
the moonlight
like polished
bone.

The bruising
loses all
colour: the
purple, green,
yellow are
shades of grey.

When she
sleeps,
she dreams
of rivers.

And
drowning.

The waters
are cool,
never cold.

Counting
the bubbles
escaping
from her
lungs, she
enjoys the
slow swirling
descent.

REBORN

By Bee Parkinson-Cameron

I thought it was going to be the last day of my life.
I'd intended it to be, that was my plan.
I had been thinking about how to do it for many years.
I had wondered what it would feel like.
Would it hurt too much?
Would I be able to bear the pain?
Would the seconds of agony pass like hours?
Would my heart be strong enough to release my soul?

I hadn't planned to do it that day when I woke up.
I had gone through the motions of my normal day.
The doldrums passing me by as the bus sped towards its destination.
It was not my final destination.
Merely a stop on my route towards my inevitable end.
When asked how I was feeling that day, I was non-committal.
My thoughts were my own, my feelings pushed deep down.
Yet on my way home, they reared their tortured head.

The feelings washed over me.
The strength of them battering my delicate body.
The water rushing into my lungs.
The darkness seeping into my heart.
The poison of the deed in my blood.
The whispers of intent whistling in my ears.
The mortal sin staining my fingers.
Staining my hands.

I took the pills.
I popped them one by one out of the packet.
The lighting was low from the lamp squatting in the corner.
There were secrets in the walls and floorboards.
I knew that this was the only option for me.
I'd wanted this for so long.
I couldn't bear my torment any longer.
I wasn't made for this world nor did I long for it.

Yet fate intervened.
I was clearly meant for more than I thought.
My attempt was a failure.
I was at the bottom, I could not fall any further than I already had.
From the darkness of the well.

I tipped my head up to the pinpoint of light.
The glowing warmth beckoned me,
In soothing tones, it promised that there was more for me.
That the life I had once owned had died.
But that I would be reborn from the ashes of my former life.
And I would be glorious.

DON'T GIVE UP

By Guy Morris

Be you rich or poor, Big or small
Suicide can often affect us all.
The pain won't end with suicide
It just passes on to another.
Your friends or parents
Your sister or brother.
"I'm Fine" you smile, to quell any concern.
But the pain that you hide, continues to burn.
All help is at hand. Do not fear to ask!
None that will help you, would class it a task.
The lives that you've touched,
The good times you've shared,
Can happen again, so please, don't be scared.
Don't give up now. Look how far you've come.
Ring, call, Talk to someone.
It's such a relief, the moment it's done.
Just knock on a door, or pick up the phone.
Trust me on this...
You're NOT on your own!

THE TORCH BEARER

By May Mathew Manoj

She was his muse, he her drug
They couldn't part in life or death
Their souls deeply connected
From the very first time they met
They couldn't let go of each other
As they were inseparable from the start

Destinies, people and all hell let loose
Yet their love blossomed unseen
Overcoming prejudices, differences and hatred
Growing stronger each day
Years passed, love flourished,concealed
Hidden from the eyes of the world

Beyond comprehension, mutual consent
Love dwelt in them, an uninvited guest
They never knew how strong their bonds were
Until one day separation knocked
Hidden love revealing itself
On the day distance knocked at their doors

Trying to forget, ignoring the pain
Yet it stabbed each other like a sharp dagger
They didn't know what it was that joined them together
Were they soul mates
Reincarnated from another lifetime?
But what did they do wrong to be so?

Sorrows of separation attacked them
Robbing them of joy, creating depression
Their eyesight clouded, panic attacks flow in
Distasteful of even their favourites
People, places, things they loved, seemed distant
Both unaware of each other's plight

Pain overtook him, her absence made him forlorn
Death giving him temporal comfort pills
She unaware of his tragedy, camouflaging pain
Spent her days caring for the needy
Until the day his desperate soul reached out to her

She felt shocked for the rest of her life.
Nothing she did could take away her hurt
No water wash away her feelings of guilt
Sometimes she wanted to end it all
To run away from her fate, suicidal thought set in
Yet, she decided each day to choose life

For she loved him enough to live for his good soul
Life became to her a daily sacrifice
Carrying the cross of sorrow
Pangs in her heart, incessant bleeding
Yet it didn't deter her from doing it for him
Now each day she lived for him, merged as one

A torch bearer of his love

ELEGY FROM A SEASIDE GRAVEYARD

By John-Karl Stokes

... and this stone-picture's Wayne, the Suicide
doing it his way: longest finger
cocked up from the earth
into the sealight fading.

Here the surfer, boy of the sea
still suckled by his mother feeling
his salt mouth, his sighing
over the tablet gravestone of the waves.

Here the incongruous, Calvinist whalers
moaning with their predestinations:
born in sin, living to lament
relieving themselves in death

and here the mother lover, with her child
still moving, on top and hung
in the harness, the smash cut
gently into the mind at twilight

and Brad, who knew Sherryl in the Biblical sense
and Nathanial who knew the smell
and ways of the mulloway. These deaths
are so Australian and yet...

The same; they are sung in the tongue
of the water, the hiss of the sandgrains
rubbing one with another,
and another, and another, under bellbirds

sounding their deathknells
into the sealight fading
So leave the dead ones to it.
They are, after all, forever.

So love them, leave them, go
pausing once, at some corner
(you will know when) ...
so Wayne, the self-killed car-hoon

when he misses you by a nail

Gives you the finger!

Resurrect your breath.

Drive on.

First published in *Fire in the Afternoon* by John-Karl Stokes (Halstead Press 2015).

EMACIATED

By Mtende Wezi Nthara

A day could not pass without imagining her chubby face
Rounded and smooth like an ostrich egg
That one could barely be seen next this eye-catcher
Fattening one whole village on consumption
She couldn't be pressed for her inescapable explosion
The kind that chiefs knelt down in prayer for
Social order couldn't but clap hands in glee
Gaiety that summoned a hangman's knot
Alligators that never marked their territory
Dawn and dusk resting on two ends of a double-edged knife
Conception of contemplation, scrutiny, cogitation
Could I go on?

Polypropylene rope? Potassium cyanide pills? Liquorice lace? Water?
Nothing is as scary as the navel-gazing
Emaciation takes over, in no time angels sing in glory.

WALK WITH ME

By Linda M. Crate

My uncle's suicide
taught me
I didn't really want to die
just wanted the pain
inside of me to wither away
wanted to carve it out
forever,
but it remains here with all these
clouds of rage that don't just blow
away in the wind;
some days are good but there are also
bad days
hard and heavy
where I feel like an anchor is wrapped
around my ankles -
I am screaming at the top of my lungs
but no one hears my pleas
for help,
and I am here trying to find ways to get the
weight off of me that is dragging me down;
some days I am successful
others I fall beneath the water choking on darkness
promising myself that tomorrow is another
day, trying to hold onto a light
I cannot see -
everyone has to save themselves,
but sometimes I think it would be nice
if someone could take the time to walk with me
because even in silence I can be content
as long as I know I am not always alone.

TRAVELLING THROUGH THE WAVES

By Pamela Scott

Stopping at the edge of the beach
she buys chips from the white van.
Saturating them in vinegar and brown sauce
she closes her eyes, tilts her head upwards
and lets the scent of the salty air fill her nostrils.

The smell of the sea fills her,
steeps into every pore. every cell
while the waves crash inside her heart.
The salt makes her nose twitch
and brings salty tears to her eyes.

Popping chips into her trembling mouth
she makes her way slowly along the beach,
hot sand scattering beneath her feet.
The sand is like fine ash between her toes
like walking on a bed of grit.

She stops dead at the water's edge,
licking vinegar and brown sauce from the bag
and sucking the bitter, sweet tag from her fingers.
Every cell, muscle in her body is tight and alert.
She listens to seagulls screeching overhead.

A crisp, cool, sea breeze blows around her.
making her raven hair whip across her face.
She feels her body turn into a block of ice.
Reaching to the sky, she spreads her arms open
and pretends she is soaring overhead. Free.

Sobbing, she peels her moist clothes off
and absently discards them on the sand.
Taking a deep breath she jumps head-first
into the ice cold water. Travelling through the waves
she lets the current drag her down. Darkness.

ROMANCING THE HOME

By Jo Wilson-Ridley

*This is for my sister Belinda who has been living with mental illness
and homelessness for 6 years. She's the bravest person I know.*

Somewhere over the rainbow
There's no place like home
Red dancing shoes won't replace
No place like home

Home is where the heart is
This home does warm my heart
Fickle from far-flung travels
Settle down, make home a start

Homeward bound
Re-joining the mind
Home for the holidays
Homecoming to one's kind

I'll be home for Christmas
Even in my dreams
Home Alone – oh my god—"Kevin"
Delight soon melts the screams

He comes— from—a good home
She comes—from—home sweet home
White wedding, white home, white picket fence
And that's the way they became a Brady home

Home sweet home
Sweet sweet was home
Home-grown, home boys
Home-town, home toys
Home brew, home born
Home movies, home porn

Home ain't what it used to be
Home ain't big enough for the two of us
Just when you thought it was safe to go back
This home is on the wrong side of the track

'Home-wrecker' she yelled
You take the home

I'm going home to Mum's…
'Cause this ain't no place like home

Between the childhood home
And the married home
Dividing the home
More or less, less home

Homeless is
The less of a home
Deep roots shallowed
When less is of your home

I don't recognise home
Where I lost my heart
Red dancing shoes faded
You knew it from the start

Homesickness strangles
Home of the brave
Come home, sweet home
Where home does save

Home
Home
Home

Interview with Jo

What prompted you to write your pieces Jo?

My writing is generated from an intense desire to understand life and the complexities of our world. Often when struggling with an aspect of life, writing provides the perspective and clarity to ingest experiences - it's through the creative expression of words I process life and what's happened to me. The two poems I've specifically written were prompted by my own experience of depression/anxiety, and also enduring depression and anxiety (and resulting homelessness) of close family. Depression/anxiety has visited me on three occasions and I am always intensely aware my family have a predisposition to depression so at any point it could return. My eldest sister had a debilitating five-year battle with depression/anxiety from 2010-2015, and there were times I experienced desperate grief watching her battle because I knew the beautiful person she was, and just wanted her to be well. During her battle my sister shared with me that she lives with suicidal thoughts and it was this brave act of sharing that I was also able to share my own similar experiences. My three bouts of depression they have also been marred by suicidal thoughts, mostly because I was so exhausted by the feelings of depression, suicide felt like a possible escape route. My sister's battle, and her commitment to wellness, has featured her sharing much of her gained wisdom including the idea that maybe we will always have suicidal thoughts in times of anxiety/depression and not be ashamed of the thoughts, just be aware of them and acknowledge them instead of being afraid of them. It was the idea of being friendly with depression, chatting and joking with it in a playful way that was the inspiration for 'Deliberations with the Black Dog'. If I could personalise depression maybe, just maybe, if it does return it'll be kind to me.

How did your depression/anxiety affect you on a daily basis?

The three times I've had depression/anxiety I've masked it. I hide it from friends and family and often endure it in silence. The first time I experienced it, was in my third year of university and it almost killed me because I suffered silently, pretending I was OK to the outside world, even though I knew I was in real trouble. I was studying Psychology and History at the time and covering subjects on depression, history of violence and child abuse - this subject matter was adding to my spiralling situation. The worst part I recall was constantly feeling a deep sense of grief and anxiety weighing me down like being smothered by a dark blanket. It was with me when I went to bed and each morning I would wake and for a brief moment I would hope, just hope it had lifted and then the feeling would descend and it would take all the remaining scrimps of energy to get out of bed and face the day. I remember sleep was the only relief from pain of depression which is where the idea started creeping in that maybe permanent sleep was the solution.

Third year of uni I was sharing a house with two friends and my brother and I was living in the attic. Because I was silently battling depression/anxiety, I had reduced life to just getting to uni and work and coming home and studying – I couldn't handle much else. I would study every night in my attic room and sleep was my only reprieve from darkness of depression. I lost faith in my ability to learn and express myself – I had essays to write for uni and I had to force myself to read old essays just to convince myself I could write and make myself start an essay. I just kept battling through.

Do you have any strong memories left of those times?

Yes, I remember once waking in the early hours of the morning and the blanket of depression was still with me. I was so tired from the darkness that I was incredibly tempted to take a bottle of sleeping pills I had and end my misery – it was an old bottle from when I'd been in hospital from a fall two years earlier. It was like the pills in the bottle were beckoning me whispering promises of relief. I remember being so scared to be alone with these thoughts that I ran out of the attic bedroom and found my brother sleeping and lay with him for two hours shaking. That had to be my darkest moment.

How do you cope any feelings of depression/anxiety you have now?

My sister has recently shared with me many great ideas of how to cope – one that I particularly love is that some days are going to feel like you're caught in a hurricane. On these days you just need to grip on and let the day wash over you knowing all you have to do is get through the day. My sister also has great strategies for bad days – a care kit featuring all your favourite small comforts to make you feel good – like your favourite bag of tea, your favourite music, a favourite poem or magazine – on bad days grab your care kit and spend fifteen minutes looking after yourself.

Do you have any advice for anyone going through similar emotions and experiences?

Don't view depression or anxiety as a failure. Own the feelings, share them, get help from family and friends and medical experts. Even go so far as to joke with them – *'You again – OK you're here but can I ask you to keep to yourself cause I gotta a life to live.'* Also, in times of wellness, read up on depression and anxiety – reading and understanding depression and anxiety has helped me appreciate the illness and ways to cope when I experience it, or when family go through it. Also, realising suicide isn't a solution to depression it closes off your chances of getting well and recovering. There's always hope.

Read Jo's other piece on page 117.

BATTLEFIELD

By Beaton Galafa

I've decided not to grant death the satisfaction he desires
He's taken one too many of my own
But I will no longer cry nor have a heavy heart
Because seeing me desolate pleases him
And he keeps coming time and again.
He saw how ruined we were when he came years ago
He saw how ruined we were when he came months ago
He saw how ruined we were when he came hours ago.
But now I will face him like the little boy in our village
Who dreamed of himself dangling from a spider web
And grabbed a rope to live his dream behind his father's house.
I want to look him in the eye when he threatens to strike again.
I want to let him know I did not go around asking for life before.
That I was an accident like himself – with different fate.
And that after here, I may have to live again.

Interview with Beaton

When did you write your two poems Beaton?

I wrote *Battlefield* in 2019 and *Sometimes* in 2018.

Can you tell me a little bit more about why you wrote them?

For *Battlefield*, it came as kind of a reaction to the news of a boy I knew in our village who had hanged himself behind his family's compound. Nobody ever knew why, but he had reminded me of a few others I knew who had decided to go by the rope, and another man who, tired of months of chronic illness, embraced death by throwing himself down an abandoned well several years back. I thought I could immortalize the boy's struggle through the poem by touching on the devastating consequences of death on the psyche of those that stay behind and the hope that comes at the thought of an afterlife.

For *Sometimes*, it came as boredom and loneliness overtook my stay in a land far from home; a land where we were all struggling to fit in and where we will leave having failed to fit in, and the struggles that have marked our stay. And on similar platforms elsewhere, I have talked about the need for a creation of our own space, especially as African students in a place that appears not to understand us as much as we would want and therefore subjecting us to, at times, to ridicule. However, for me I wouldn't say that there has ever been a struggle I can label as reaching crisis levels.

As I wrote the two poems, albeit at different times and inspired by different events, there were recurring images of souls that have found in death permanent relief, and at some point I remembered a policeman in Zomba (a city in the south in Malawi) who, having endured the sight of his chronically ill sister – they were the only ones remaining in their family - went missing one day in 2017, only to be found in a nearby forest later hanging from a tree. The sister collapsed on hearing the devastating news and never recovered; they were buried on the same day. I was at the time living in the neighbourhood where the man was found dead. It is in honour of such people that I believe it so happened that I had to write these two poems.

Do you have anything to say to anyone thinking about ending their lives in such a way?

To those who would be going through experiences that bring them closer to thoughts of liberating themselves through death, I might not have anything special to say aside from giving life one more chance when on the verge of giving up. They should focus on the positives of this life, and the people – even if there is just one – who will have to go through similar torture as they went through at the thought of their departure. They should know there is always a moment – there will always be – of redemption. It's this hope that keeps us all going; we are all fighting our own battles, some of which we will never win, yet we still have to find a way out, alive. It's not as easy as I say, but that's how we all survive. And we must always share stories of our struggles with friends and family; those we trust, those who can understand, and even those we aren't sure will understand. We can make them understand by sharing the pain. What's more important? To us, everyone, everyday; we've got to keep checking on our friends and family and we should listen with our hearts and offer help that we would ourselves love to get if we were to be in similar situations. There are times we've joked about death and life, about suicide and eternity, about better alternatives yet what we tend to ignore is the psychological state of the suicidal, and how our very existence would be of much importance to their survival through such devastating moments.

Read Beaton's other piece on page 188.

REPETITION
By Parvinder Kaur

So mum, here I am repeating it all again
A little stressed, a little in pain.
I didn't think it would come to this ever again.
Didn't think I was strong enough to bare the pain.
But here I am, again in the same place tonight.
Like last night. And the night before that night.

To take out the blade I use up all my might.
And then I roll up my sleeve and bring my canvas to sight.

I draw passionately.
I try curves.
I try straight lines.

But of course in a while it starts to hurt.
The pain grows and the blood won't stop to flow.

Mom I wish you were here.
To hold me while I cry.
Why is that when one of us goes through something,
The other one is at stand by.

It is difficult to see.
How blind we've become.
Come, lets hold each other,
Before we go numb.

CONSTANTLY AWAY

By Noor Yousif

The sun dimmed
Eternal gloom
I embraced my wails
I have been pushed away
Hidden bitterness beneath wrath
Get away, bury your gasp

Weary entity in the way
Passive tempest seemed to never go away

Along despair
I stumbled in dismay
Nothing seems to go away

Obey your fear
Don't wipe your tears away
You're doomed invariably to live away

From chasm to abyss
You will always be away

MISTY VENEER

By Pasithea Chan

I stood alone like a blank page
listening to my life shoot blanks
from behind a veneer so misty with Jeer.
And as my tears rained down
pain's pane my soul took a dive.
I dropped my heart on its head
cracking it open to face a sneer.

That was reality spilling tragedy
from my life like a cup of coffee
into my blank eyes that sank deeper
in sorrow until I became hollow.
I watched loved ones tumble away
without a hey or are you okay.
In the end sadness became my only friend
and living a game of pretend.

It's always raining outside my veneer
that's why my mind is never clear.
Sometimes my voice breaks and
life gives blunt aches with no brakes.
There are only echoes behind my veneer
nothing grows there but woes
placed carefully with sharp edges
that cut with blues without queues.

Sometimes I stick my face close
to the veneer and breath on its glass
trying to see if there's life left in this
lass via breaths and maybe warmth.
Everything is gloomy outside,
even weeds tumble in pairs only I am alone.
Mirth is something I will only know
after death that will set me free finally.

So for now I stand behind my misty veneer
reminiscing all those I lost and held dear.
I have no fear having lived with one who lived to tear
my soul with words sharper than a pair of rusty shears.
So here I am standing behind my misty veneer
waiting for my finale to set me free

from this world of tears.

Author's Notes: İnspired by Life: *"Why do people love me but hate you?"* Death: *"Because you are a beautiful lie and am a painful truth."*

ALL OF THE OLD RITUALS

By Pamela Scott

All of the old rituals;

reading a favourite poem, a page of prose,
alphabetising lists in my head, wearing
mismatched socks, only stepping on
every 3rd stone on the road,
making up a new playlist –

even the touch and smell of my lover's skin,
salted caramel hot chocolate (with cream),
the hot sun on my face

have started to fail,
their old magic has faded,
come to nothing

the old rituals have abandoned me

the darkness is back, stronger
then ever, pushing into the
softest, deepest parts of me

I can hardly breathe

I feel her, my old enemy,
clawing at my throat,
her hand covers my mouth,
suffocates me

her voice whispers poison
in my ear, turns every good
thought black until it rots in me

after all these years,
of fighting back, keeping
the bitch at bay

a part of me wants to succumb

DARE

By Ebuwa Ohenhen

Today I was drenched by the rain on my way home.
I was reminded of the number of times
I've drenched my heart in pain.
I was taken back in time
to the signs on the wall,
Signs I ignored.

Where were you when I was drowning?
Where were you when I fought for my sanity?
Where were you when I lost?

You're the pain that has
been eating me up inside.
You're my greatest enemy.

Am I weak?
I was,
but not anymore.
Am I strong?
I didn't used to be,
But I am now.

So come, I dare say,
Whatever pain thou art,
Come and thou shalt find me ready.

Come, you faceless coward!
I shan't be stabbed from the back anymore
I'm not afraid of thy sting.
I am the antidote to my own pain,
Thy shackles no longer have any hold on me.
This isn't like ol' times,
For today I dare to fight.
I will win.

ACHE

By Abigail George
(for the Dutch poet Joop Bersee)

You're like a wet taproot burrowing-digging-digging
into the ground. You're flinch, a flicker and a burn.
You're desolate. You know you are and you will not
be triumphant today. My wish is to outlive England.
I have spent these lonely years, all these aching hours
knowing you. The loss and feeling, the animal-murmur
of my weeping, and residue of this stubborn mental
fight. My feet walk in Egypt, Jerusalem, Syria, the jungles
of Africa. My feet find trails, float on paths of cobblestone

and asphalt jungle. My legs turn green in the sea. My last
breath will come I know in time. Where I am going to
I don't know that for sure. The white picket fences of
heaven or the territories of hell. I am armed with neither
the light of love or the reward of joy. I think of the clashing-
hungry-roaring sea. I think of the startled fight, fright,
flight and adrenaline of self-harm. I think of the struggle
that lounges there. You, cutting, are as desolate as the shore
as I've said before. You paint me utterly ape, and bird,

peacock and parrot, animal and amethyst. You paint me
with age, with rage. You're so various, so complex, so-
complicated with genteel-loneliness, and talk self-harm. You're
so newfound. You've been found dying before. I have. I
have. I have. You took those pills and fell in moonlight, the
green grass glowing, the quietness stirring in the dark. You
can only think of self-harm in the dark. Thoughts of suicide
and self-harm are no stranger to me. They come like thunder
ripping me apart, tearing me apart. I sleep now in the glory,

the glow (always the glow of green grass in the moonlight or
in the daylight). I can't stand to self-harm, to cut in daylight.
Better the night. The night is better. I'm lying on my back
on my bed in high care in the ward. I remember everything.
I remember nothing. I think of York, Sussex and Nottingham. No
reason do I have to fear York, Sussex and Nottingham. Yes,
England, you puritan, I think I will outlive you. Hold my hand.
Please just hold onto my hand. Look! My legs turn green in
the seawater. I think of you now and then suicide. Much too

scared to dive in wholeheartedly. Much too frightened even
to attempt you again. You're a ghost that will haunt me to the end
of my days in this world until I find the other side of paradise.
I think of you as dull now and far-gone forever and ever and
ever. I think of you as I think of a frozen river, a winter river.
Flow river, flow to the sea. Forgive me. Forgive me for thinking
of taking my own life. Farewell river. Farewell cutting.
Farewell self-harm. Farewell your splendid towers and spires
and cathedrals. I'm done with you. I bid you adieu, adieu, adieu!

CHECKMATE. GAME OVER

By Barbara Hawthorn

TO WHOM IT MAY CONCERN.

I am writing this at 12.45pm on Wednesday the 24th. I came home at midday after my weekly chess encounter at Dave Todd's. (A draw today, and no time for a decider). Thinking back it was odd the house was so quiet. No table set for lunch. No Emma pottering in the kitchen.

I went straight to the bathroom, dying to pee. And I just didn't see her. I can't believe I didn't see her. I was so urgently focussed. It was only after I flushed and turned round that I saw her. Correction. My eyes saw. But my brain refused to understand the message. Oh Emma. She was already grey and turning blue. Cold fingers when I took her hand. Cold lips when I kissed her.

She had padded the bottom of the bath tub with towels and rested her head on the pillow from her bed. On her lap was a collection of empty pill bottles and a scattering of spilled tablets. Oh Emma. I don't know how long I knelt there, numb at the side of the tub. Eventually I staggered back to the kitchen and saw the notes she had left. Two sealed envelopes addressed to Rebecca and Tom, and a sheet for me. It was a short message: "Sorry darling. I just can't go on any more". She didn't need to explain; she had been suffering from clinical depression. The doctor monitoring her had prescribed antidepressants. Well, too bad Doc, but they just didn't work. Oh Emma. I should never have left you. What was I thinking? Was I thoughtfully leaning over the chessboard, chin on hand, pondering my next move, at the very moment you climbed into the tub?

There are stamps as usual in the little brass box; Emma is - oh, was – always so well organised. So I will go and post Rebecca's letter in a moment. It won't take me long. I won't post Rob's: what's the point. He's overseas. I will leave his here with this message. To whom it may concern. Sorry Rebecca, I guess it will be you. I will leave the key in the door. My affairs are more or less in order. Our wills are with Hammond and Lewis, on the corner of Main and Stewart.

When I come back from the post box, I will use more towels to make myself a pad to lie on – the tiled floor is cold and hard. Right beside my Emma. I too have a stash of pills: heart stuff mainly. She has a head start, but maybe I can catch up with her and we can go on this journey together. Oh Emma. Why did you do this? To whom it may concern. What am I saying? Rebecca, it will be you? Please know, I just can't go on without my Emma.

Forgive me.

FIFTY

By Hannah Louise MacFarlane

They call this a crime, the feeling that flutters in my chest and threatens to break free into a murmuration of loose words and half empty promises of weddings and travelling the world that my pecuniary vices must snicker at as I speak.

They call it a sin, but I swear to every god, deity and other worldly force that dares to listen that this is the most heavenly experience of my life. Nothing about the way I love her feels damnable, but if it is then I will succumb to the flames with pride.

They call it a lie, that these feelings are my mind playing tricks on me and as if being in love was the same as my depression. My depression makes me want to die, and she is at the top of the list of reasons to stay alive, the two have never met once so the comparison of the two is a tragedy, because my sickness should never be compatible with my happiness.

Half of us are statistically going to die. The L should stand for listen, I swear we aren't trying to hurt you with our authenticity. I understand your social perceptions are telling you to be disgusted by me, but my love is as true as yours and if you've never loved like this then don't ruin me for not being like you.

Half of us are statistically going to die. The G should stand for grief, not for the death of something tangible but for the death of progress for those before, after and around us. Losing life to bigotry only feeds the hate but it's hard to dictate to someone who has buried their son that their loss was not due to a community, but due to a broken, ancient hypocrisy.

Half of us are going to die. The B should stand for beauty, the kind that exists when people come together instead of being torn apart and give way to flexibility. Progress is not progress without power and power only exists when there are people brave enough to believe in something bigger than themselves. The powerful notion of equality is the only thing brave enough to save us all.

Half of us are going to die. The T should stand for tragedy, when none of these words are heard and there's no life but so many bodies. When each stripe of the rainbow is brought down by hate, and there lies half of our fates. My friend, my foe, my once facebook friend, it no longer matters. In a row of ten, only five of these young lives will matter. Five of those lives will be cut short, for no noble cause, for no wars, for no lives saved, simply because that was the fate forced on them by a lack of tolerability.

Half of us are going to die. The + should be left alone. Plus what? Plus who? Plus, what makes your opinion so true? In a sea of keyboard warriors, cyber stalkers and locker room talkers, fifty percent of the LGBT+ community will take their own lives to escape the insanity. To escape constant masquerades and wrong sex dates. To escape being mis-gendered, misunderstood, mistaken, and murdered. Half of us are going to die, by our own hands, because of theirs.

They are everywhere. Hidden in shadows, in crowded rooms, there is no place for homophobia to hide. Except from coffins of those their words have killed, and funerals of children who took their own lives because they were told being in love was more distasteful than being alive.

SUICIDE
By Robin Barratt

Shall I drive my car into the wall,
or jump into a lake,
or leap from a tall building,
or slit my wrists?

Shall I overdose on sleeping tablets,
or inject myself with heroin,
or I step out in front of a train,
or hang myself from a tree?

Shall I stab myself with a knife,
or drink rat poison,
or set myself on fire,
or jump from the pier?

Shall I gas myself in the car,
or put a plastic bag over my head,
or inject air into my veins,
or drink a few bottles of vodka

I want to die, but I just don't know how.

Published in the forthcoming *Naked in the Rain* by Robin Barratt.

JUST ASK

By Sarah Clarke

Clouds drift gently by
A breeze sends them on their way
Oblivious to the turmoil in my mind
A fight leaving friends at a loss what to say

The bench etches its imprint on my back
Reminding me I am here
Alive, feeling, trying to still the inner chaos
Its support tells me I have nothing to fear

Yet I fall further, more lost than ever
Puzzled by the pounding in my chest
Steadfast, strong, calling me back
Urging me to stay, your heart knows what's best

The rumble of distant trucks draws me away
A hypnotic sound offering me a way to vanish
I wonder who drives, what and where
Their gigantic wheels a solution to my anguish

Shocked by the finality of this idea
I am suddenly more present than ever
Momentarily the anxiety subsides
Long enough for thought of that option to sever

I hurry away from the road
Pound on door after door
For months searching for help
The internal wounds still raw

Friends know something is amiss
Yet believe I am invincible
It couldn't be true of me so no one asks
While I wonder; why am I suddenly invisible?

I find support
A year goes by and I am well
My mind under control
A story ready to tell

Sometimes I think back to that dark place

Had I disappeared that day
Would friends standing heads bowed think
We never knew what to do or say?

A friendly smile, a drink to share
A gentle word or two or three
A place to connect, to be and feel safe
That was all I needed of thee

Nothing more complicated than that
A chance to rediscover life's joys
Without these simple things I almost left
Jumping off the world to stop the noise

HOW MANY TIMES DID I CRY TODAY?

By Pamela Scott

The first tears fall
when I have a stupid
argument with my lover.

An innocent remark,
misinterpreted. I find
myself sniping,
quick to anger and tears.

The second tears
come when I'm
finally told, after
two weeks that
I didn't get a job
I interviewed for,
that I really wanted.

I feel tears of frustration;
anger,
self-pity,
disappointment,
resignation
and defeat.

The third tears
fall, unexpectedly
in the toilets.
I'm not thinking or
feeling anything
in particular.

A wave of
sadness sweeps
over me, so
intense it stops
my breath. I
feel my face
fall apart
and the sobs
shake me.

I cry like
a child
and cover my
face with
both hands.
My mouth trembles,
the sadness fills
every inch of me.

I'm on
the verge
of tears all
day, sorrow
simmers below
the surface.

*I just want to
lie in a dark
room, hug myself
and rock.*

And I don't even know why.

DESOLATE REDEMPTION

By Pasithea Chan

Listening to nothing in my ribcage
I see the void growing deep within

Playing catch with blame and misery
I bleed sense unto past memories.

I am machine a part of me is a soldier
enlisted to serve broken dreams.

Wrestling the present to push through
I am pinned down with things I cant change

Should I put my guns down and call -
for truce hoping for release from this pain?

It is a beautiful pain compared to the void-
lurking in a future shining with distrust.

Every step I take seems like a blow -
that leaves me to spat my soul on and on.

I wish I can say goodbye to the dark
I wish I can witness sunrise but am stuck.

All I have are broken pieces and fragments -
of questions never answered.

I can't find the reason for all this chaos.
So I keep wishing for a miracle.

Seems like a ritual of everlasting agony-
and so my search for desolate redemption goes on.

WOUNDS

By Bee Parkinson-Cameron

Time can heal all wounds
That's what I've always been told,
But some wounds are too deep
Becoming a fading scar when I'm old.

I have a masochistic nature,
Pain just feels good somehow.
It hurts at first then the pulsing,
Reminds me of every feeling now

The anger courses through my veins,
In my very blood it burns.
Nails and teeth and blades they stroke,
Slowly but surely, pain's ways she learns.

The anger, it's always there,
The desire to punish the world and self.
A walking jury I have become,
Each hour a drain on my health.

Sometimes I need to control my body
Sometimes I do it for power.
Sometimes I do it to feel,
Yet always the action tastes sour.

There are some other reasons,
My thoughts and feelings are in my blood.
If I let it seep out, they're drained,
I begin to change with the seasons.

I don't know why I've become this way,
It wasn't how I grew up.
When I was younger I used to frolic,
Now blood is the only game I play.

This world has let me pass by,
Enjoying my masks through rose glasses.
The marks remind me who I am,
Lest I should believe my own crafted lie.

BETTER LATE THAN NEVER

By David A Banks

I recognised the look on the students face as
he apologised, with a dead flat voice,
for his assignment being late.

I studied him carefully.
A typical student; young, naive
but, unlike most, no spark in his eyes.

He listened, deafly, to my words
then rose to leave, promising the assignment tomorrow.

Or perhaps next week.

> *My mind went back to...*

I asked him if he would mind going to the counselling service.
No remonstrations. No denial. A shrug and 'OK'

> *I was right*

I rang the counsellors – an appointment in a few days time?
I looked at his face again.
No, I said, it must be today. In fact, I'll send him to you right now.

I told him that the counsellor would see him now
and told him where to go.
He nodded and was half way through the doorway ...

> *Damn memories*

... when I said I'd walk along with him.
No, it's no trouble I said.

We walked along South Terrace in silence
as the bright blue jacaranda blossom swirled around us.
What could we possibly have talked about?

> *And I remembered days long ago in another life when I joked*
> *"If you slit your wrists in the bathroom you can clean up the*
mess".

I left him when he entered the door to the counsellors office.

At least, I thought, I may see him again.

THERE IS A GUN ON THE TABLE

By Mike Rollins

Something swells
Inside me
Dark, full of
Longing

There is a
Gun on
The table

You are almost
Here, but not
Quite

I am almost
There

Because
There is a
Gun on
The table

And the world
Is too much
Without
You

DELIBERATIONS WITH THE BLACK DOG

By Jo Wilson-Ridley

Should we meet again...
Let's pretend to be long lost friends
air kisses through gritted smiles
promising to stay in contact;
then stride away
eyes fixed straight

Should we meet again...
Let's tango like estranged lovers
holding our heads high
remaining at arm's length
we won't linger; a quick elevator chat
before the lift door shuts

Should we meet again...
Let's duel like western outlaws
start back to back
guns raised to the heavens
and never stop counting
as we step further apart

Should we meet again...
Let's engage in a bullfight
I'll be the proud Matador side-stepping
your horns with a ballerina's grace;
our dalliance cut short, from my
first blow piercing your heart

Should we meet again...
Let's agree to give fair warning
arrive bearing gifts of flowers and chocolates
stay a mere day and leave silently through the night
I'll learn of your departure reading your
'Dear Dog' letter - left on my pillow

Previously published by *fourWtwenty-seven New Writing An Anthology of Prose & Poetry* by Booranga Writers Centre, fourWpress, Wagga Wagga, November 2016.

TO GIVE A THING A NAME

By Pamela Scott

I've always felt this way:
up and down, intense,
moving from one extreme
emotion to another,
bursting into tears for
nothing, quick to anger
and quick to tears.

I never knew not everyone
felt this way.

I never knew there
was a word for this

D E P R E S S I O N

SAD

By Bill Cox

Winter closes in around me
Like the walls of a dark pit.
Life becomes monochrome,
Devoid of colour.
I try to climb out,
But in my mind I feel hands grasping
Clawing
Pulling me down,
Down.
Into the black recesses
I fall,
Into that horrid singularity
I tumble,
Where dreadful thoughts
Embrace me
With
Their
Suffocating
Inescapable
Gravity.

ETERNAL WINTER

By Linda M. Crate

I didn't know he was suffering
or the magnitude of his pain,
and depression isn't something
you can just get over;
but I remember you saying you didn't
understand why he couldn't
just get over it -
I know it must have been frustrating
to see him going through
all the pain,
not being able to reach him with your love
he was your brother;
and yet I find I relate to him more than I do you
there are secrets in our souls
we are afraid of all the things that may bring
those we love shame so we bury them deep inside
praying that we don't leave behind
a tell -
I wish our love could've saved him,
that our tears weren't falling like the rain
on the day of his funeral;
I wish that the sun could've reached him burning away
the winter that lingered in his heart
I wish for him a summer could have come.

PTSD

By Richard Goss

PTSD is my life.
My life has never
been simple, always pain and grief
Never a normal life.
All I want to do is hurt myself,
and be free from the pain and grief in life.
Even though everything is good,
it is so hard to be normal.
People think I make it up,
but I really don't.
I just don't know how to say it out allowed
as they don't understand.
My head is like a washing machine;
it goes round and round.
When will it end?
Should I cut myself?
Should I just jump off a bridge?
Should I hang myself?
Should I take a overdose?
It is selfish, I know,
but I don't like my mind on days like this.

I DO NOT WANT YOUR SYMPATHY

By Malcolm Judd

I do not want your sympathy
Nor do I need you to understand,
All I ask is you show a little empathy
When depression takes my hand.

Do not cross the road to avoid my path
Or whisper so that I may not hear,
I only want a chat and a laugh
My friendship to still be held dear.

The illness which lies deep within my mind
Cannot be seen by you or anyone,
But take the time to talk, do not be blind
Do not be scared of me please do not run.

I do not want to lose my family my friends
Just because of my mental health,
The deep dark hole into which I descend
Cannot be filled with luxury or wealth.

So next time you see me please say *hi*
It may not be as scary as you may think,
I will be honest with you and never lie
A friend is all I need so that I may not sink.

Interview with Malcolm

Why did you write your poem Malcolm?

If you read between the lines of my poem, you will find a person who has suffered many years, lost many friends and sadly some family due to my mental health; that is why I wrote the poem and that is why I now try to help other people who suffer from the same mental health issues.

From losing my father at aged five, to losing my first wife at twenty, from being bullied at school and at work, my whole life has been a psychological nightmare. There have been numerous times where I have wanted to just give up, and yet there have also been many times when I have felt inspired and ready to face the world.

Through all of my life I have wanted to help people, whether that be in a physical way or a psychological one. It has been my goal since recovering from my long fight with depression, and it will always be my goal for as long as I am alive; to help people understand mental health and to remove the terrible stigma which still surrounds this illness.

Is it easy asking for help?

No, admitting you need help is often the hardest of all steps to take, but generally the first step on the road to recovery. Of course some people will refuse to help, but what a lot of people do not understand - or maybe cannot grasp - is the effect poor mental health has on the person suffering, and their loved ones. There is also a stigma surrounding men showing their emotions; it is still frowned upon and for a man, being depressed is seen as a sign of weakness. But this is not true; if someone is depressed it does not mean they are weak. Some people suffer depressions due to life events, whereas other have depression because of chemical imbalances in their brain. For some it is like a black cloud which sits over their head and that they are always being rained on. For others it could seem like they are worthless and do not fit into society, either because they choose a different lifestyle to which their family and friends have adopted, or maybe it is just because they are unable to express themselves like everyone else. There are so many different types of depressive illnesses.

How did depression affect you?

I suffered clinical depression from 1984 to 2010, and again recently from September 2018. I was not diagnosed, however, until 1996; it was only then I realised I had actually suffered from depression for many years previously. I was told my depression was due to the losses I had suffered; my father when I was just five, and the fact that one Saturday morning I had woken up to my young wife of just eighteen months of marriage dead. When I was in my lowest of low moods, I would stay indoors, and make excuses not to go out, which would become very frustrating for people close to me because they were unable to accept that I was not well.

How else did depression affect you?

Work suffered; I would feign an illness so I could have a day off just because I was unable to face another day but the problem however, was when I was due to return to work the following day, my anxiety would make me panic and I would find another excuse not to go, or get someone to call for me saying I was still unwell. This happened often resulting in me either losing or leaving my job. The benefit system was such that I would be able to stay out of work as long as my doctor wrote me sick notes and there were times I would literally beg my doctor to write me off for a month, because I just couldn't face going back into society and living a normal life and would panic with the fear that my doctor would say I was okay to return to work. Once I had to attend a medical for my benefit to continue and had to score 12 points for me to stay off work, I scored 11. My benefit was stopped, including my rent and council tax help and I had to go back to work. I lasted three months or so and then it all started again.

How did things get worse?

I found myself at the bottom of a very deep pit and one day took what little money I had and bought a dozen boxes of pain killers and two litres of vodka and took everything. If it had not been for a passer-by I would not be here. I spent three days on life support, and was discharged.

Did things change after that?

I thought to myself, why have I been doing this to myself? Was I to blame for my father dying? No. Was I to blame for my wife passing away ? No. Then why was I punishing myself? I stayed with friends for three months until I became a little stronger and a bit more stable, then moved back home and started to rebuild my life. I found a cleaning job in a cricket club. I also started working the club's bar. Then I did some maintenance work, when someone asked if I could paint their fence, which I did. Then more people asked me if I could do jobs for them, and within three months I had started a little business which ran for six years. I had survived. I had been given another chance and I was not going to waste it this time.

SEARCHING

By Bee Parkinson-Cameron

The smash and shatter of fragile dreams,
could be heard several offices away.
The workers marching like ants
pause and lift antennas high; searching.

Home-makers and mothers, the hardiest breed,
they hear the wail of a lost child,
and they look now too, like meerkats,
searching for the lost one; wailing.

The homeless wrapped in soiled possessions
that they traded their morals to own,
they hear a tinkling, a ringing like the phone
in the box across the street where their families are searching.

The children playing, swinging in the trees,
they hear a shrill scream, like an injured friend.
Their hair stands on end and they stop and
rise, looking as though they have been called; searching.

The reality of what has happened
is far worse than mere wails and dreams.
Every sound heard is combined now in one,
blending with rage and fear for frantic screams.

They search and search, then they stop.
No more searching, now they have found it.
They wish they could hide,
eyes closed, to forget what they have seen, but it is futile.

Heads hang low now, in memory of the unknown.
Clothes are tattered and shredded,
the strips falling down with the glass,
as the flag of bloodied flesh flutters slowly in the breeze.

COMMENCING

By Parvinder Kaur

When my tears dry up
Eyes unfocused, nerves mess up.
Then I abuse me.

TREADING ON EGGSHELLS

By Pamela Scott

I don't need you to feel sorry for me,
give each other sympathetic looks across
the top of my slightly bent head
or talk around me in whispers.

I'd appreciate it if you didn't
talk about me in the third person
as if I don't really exist at all
and am not sitting directly in front of you.

I refuse to talk about what happened
using abbreviations and acronyms
as if using a pretend name
will make it less real somehow.

I'd prefer if you didn't huddle in the corner,
look at me over your shoulder
and talk in hushed tones.

I'll never refer to my actions
as my *recent trouble* or
that *situation* or my *mishap*.

Please call it what it is and shame the devil.

Please don't be afraid to call me
that girl who tried to kill herself

That girl's me.
I'm her.

You don't need to speak to me in a
condescending tone,
the kind you'd use
on a misbehaving child.

I refuse to answer endless questions
about my *state of mind*.
I'll never be able to make you understand.

Why do you talk down to me

as if you're superior
and I'm just a weak
child who needs coddling?

I won't be psycho-analysed
or look at inkblots or whatever.

I don't work that way.

You can ask me,
face-to-face what I was
doing the night I tried
to end my life.

It's okay to speak
about what happened.
You won't set me off again.

There's no need to lock the knife drawer,
padlock the medicine cabinet,
put bars on all the windows
or supervise me 24-7.

Please refrain from getting up every hour
to check on me during the night
just to make sure I'm sound asleep.

Please don't shelter me
from the big bad world.

I'm not a child.

I don't need to be looked after.

I'm not a fragile piece of glass
who'll shatter into a thousand fragments
if you so much as glance in my direction.

This wasn't a cry for help.

I rarely cry and I don't need your help.

I don't do the damsel in distress bit.

I'm not that kind of girl.

Don't tread around me on eggshells.

I don't need your sympathy.

I just need to be left alone.

ESHA'S JOURNEY TO THE POINT OF SUICIDE AND BACK

By Shereen Abraham

The words Live and Die have only one 'I' but the word Suicide has two 'I's' – as I sat down to write this piece I wondered why. Could it be because that in suicide there is a stress on 'I' and the way 'I' feel... how am 'I' surviving in this world, why am 'I' being treated like this by others, why am 'I' unable to cope with life, why am 'I' being punished for no fault of mine, what have 'I' done to deserve this or what can 'I' do to make it better for me?

I have had the blessing of working with different people and bringing them up from the depths of despair. I have witnessed minds that were filled with gloom, blossoming; minds that were filled with negativity, looking for the positives; and minds that were wallowing in self-pity become confident. I would like to share the story of one of them.

We will call her Esha (name has been changed to protect her identity). Esha grew up in India and had a blissful childhood. She was always the smart kid, the well brought-up child who made her parents proud while growing up. Enthusiastic about everything that she did, Esha had big dreams for her future. Her parents always encouraged her to explore her varied interests, blaze her own trail and find her true calling. After graduating from university, she started working at one of the top luxury lifestyle companies in the country. She moved quickly up the corporate ladder, as was expected for someone like her. When Esha felt it was the right time, she got married and very soon became the mother to a beautiful baby boy. She immersed herself in the joys of motherhood and her small family of three was as happy as could be.

A couple of years later, Esha's husband got an offer to move to the Middle East on a job that seemed heaven sent. Esha had to sadly quit the job she really enjoyed and move to the Middle East, to start a new life in a place that she had only read about in the books and seen in the movies. Life in the Middle East was very different for Esha as compared to her life in India. It was not just the cultural change, it was also a lifestyle change, because a few months after the move Esha realized that her husband's job was not really "heaven sent" as they were given to understand. Slowly things started falling apart. The husband being extremely stressed at work, would come home and be the most unpleasant version of himself with Esha and their son. He found fault with everything that Esha did or did not! Their happy little world had been shattered with her husband's unreasonable angry outbursts, irritability, sarcasm and scorn. The negativity slowly started eating into her. The once vivacious lady was now a quiet, sad person with low self-esteem. Her smile never reached her eyes, her laughter was forced, her appetite was poor and her energy levels were low.

When she first came to see me, Esha was an emotionally broken woman with neither the hope nor the strength to believe that her life could change for the better. During the course of therapy Esha told me she often wondered why her husband was verbally abusing her whenever he came back home stressed from work. At first she tried to be the sponge to his unreasonable outbursts, but as time went by it became increasingly difficult to shut out the negativity. The negative energy at home was also badly affecting their son, his health and his studies. Esha's tormented mind tried to find avenues to make this better. Nothing seemed to work anymore. She was now a very pale version of her bright and chirpy self. She told me that the thought of ending her life came to her mind several months before, but something seemed to be holding her back. How did a smart, educated, forward-thinking woman come to this conclusion? Why was suicide the answer? Why was it not prayers? Why was it not couple counselling? Why was it not a lot of other things?

When one chooses to end his/her own life, it also has a lot to do with courage; that momentary courage that one needs to actually commit the act. The irony of it all – it takes a lot of courage to kill oneself, but to everyone else it may seem that the one who is contemplating suicide (or has committed suicide) is the least courageous of all. To the others, the mind had perhaps come to that decision due to a lack of courage in standing up for what is right. Esha's emotional state led her to believe that suicide was the only answer to end her woes. By this time, her tormented mind was working like a movie script writer to find the best way to commit the act in a country far, far away from her native land. Esha also wondered what might happen, if she was not successful at her first suicide attempt. Would she be jailed for attempting suicide as it was a criminal act under the local laws? Despite that, suicide to her seemed the answer to end her pain and to make the life of the one responsible for bringing her to this state live in regret for the rest of his life. Through it all, Esha wished she could rewind her life and turn back the pages of time. But whenever she jogged down memory-lane, it caused her to have dangerous mood swings. Esha grew more and more despondent.

For Esha it took one step at a time to come out from the depths of despair and fly high once again. She is completely healed and is now shining brighter than she did before. One of my favourite quotes by Dr. Wayne Dyer comes to mind; *"If you change the way you look at things, the things you look at change."* It is not easy, but in my personal experience it is worth trying, because it can make a big difference.

Interview with Shereen

Tell me a little bit about your piece Shereen.

They say that the mind is like water. When it's turbulent, it is difficult to see, but when it's calm everything becomes clear. Sometimes the turbulence leads one down a very dark path at the end of which they believe, is the point of no return. So why do people end up going down the dark path? The reasons are aplenty, but in my experience the most common one is low self-esteem. We may not be aware of it, but our self-esteem influences our daily life – the choices we make, the way we behave in new situations, how we appear to other people and the way we interact with those around us.

When does this low self-esteem start?

It starts from our childhood – the way we were treated by our parents, our siblings, our teachers, our friends and our extended family members. The way we were treated as children echoes well into our adulthood. An event or a series of events that happened in the past could lead to one having low self-esteem.

Can you explain what is self-esteem?

Self-esteem reflects the overall emotional evaluation of yourself. It may be totally positive, or positive with some doubt; it may be partly negative or totally negative. When it is totally negative, the dangers of going down the dark path seem facile.

From your experience what drives people to that dark path?

In my experience there are a few reasons that are common among the people who reach the brink of suicide.

- Their life seems empty and meaningless.
- They have nothing to look forward to in life and are extremely pessimistic about the future.
- They feel unwanted, unloved or lonely.
- They have self-loathing and believe that no one would care or miss them if they died.
- They seem to have only bad days.
- Everything around them seems to be negative.

And again, from your experience, what sort of people have

you come across that have considered suicide, and why?

- Someone who was in an abusive verbal and physical relationship, thought suicide was a better option than moving out of the relationship.

- Someone who always scored the highest marks in class, thought suicide was better than being the one who scored slightly less than the highest marks.

- Someone who was a beautiful woman both inside and out, thought suicide was the only option when her partner cheated on her with a stunner of loose morals.

- Someone who was fit and healthy always, thought of suicide when diagnosed with a disease that would leave blotchy, blemishes all over his body.

- Someone who played and earned very well in the stock market, contemplated suicide when a huge chunk of his earnings were wiped off one day. His reasoning – his inability to downgrade his high-society life style!

The Buddha said; "*The mind is everything. What you think you become.*" Just as healthy food and exercise is important to maintain a healthy body, thinking positive and consciously nurturing positivity is important for a healthy mind. The value one attribute's to oneself can make a big difference.

How does self-esteem affect someone, and how can it be improved?

Your self-esteem, or how you value yourself as a person, affects your mind, body and relationships. Now, because positive self-esteem is both a cause and a result of healthy living, you can take steps to improve your self-esteem just as you can learn to change unhealthy habits. Remember though that change takes time and is an ongoing process. During the initial days your self-esteem can go up or down, so it may help to keep a daily journal to track your progress. With practice, you will start recognizing negative thought habits and its adverse effects. However, self-esteem should not to be confused with self-respect; the two concepts may seem similar but the differences between them are crucial. Self-esteem is based on what you think, while self-respect is based on what you do. Self-respect requires you to accept how others feel about you. Self-esteem values your feelings about yourself. Developing a strong sense of self-respect can help you fulfil your potential, while developing positive self-esteem can help improve the quality of your life.

And this stems from childhood?

Yes, the successes and failures we experienced early in our lives often shape our attitudes towards achievement. Remember learning to skip or to hula-hoop or to cycle or to swim? You may have experienced many failed attempts before experiencing the joy of succeeding in doing it well. Do you remember your first stage performance? Were you speechless with stage-fright or confidently performing your part? Did you forget the lines midway and wish that the earth would open up and swallow you? Depending on whether you persevered till you succeeded or ran away, can almost accurately indicate how you would handle a tough job interview, pitch for a project, make a presentation at work, handle a heartbreak or negotiate life's many ups and downs, in your later years. A child who is loved, supported and encouraged will develop a healthy self-esteem. On the contrary if a child is constantly ridiculed or abused will suffer terribly from low self-esteem and may risk growing up to be a dangerous and destructive human being.

How important is it to have good self-esteem?

It is essential to have a healthy and positive self-esteem as it leads to being self-confident... and being self-confident is hugely important because it affects every aspect of our lives. Many people struggle to find self-confidence in themselves and this can end up being a vicious circle for them, because if self-confidence is their shortcoming, then they will find it difficult to become successful. Even from a health and well-being perspective having positive self-esteem is desirable, because when you feel good about yourself:

- You radiate positive energy.
- Your moods will be balanced.
- You will be happy communicating with others.
- You will feel empowered to take on challenges.
- You will be able to accept criticism.
- You will be able to deal skilfully with stressful situations.
- You will make healthy choices in life and,
- You will appreciate your life.

So right now who you believe you are is who you are, because nothing is more important than how you feel and think about yourself. Sadly, in today's society not many people love themselves for who they are or what they do, because subconsciously they are comparing themselves to others.

Can you learn self-esteem and self-confidence?

Fortunately, yes, one can learn to become self-confident and actually change the way your life is lived. If you are a confident person you will inspire confidence in those around you and gaining the confidence of those around you is key to finding success. The changes that you could make are often tiny as compared to the enormous positivity it can bring to your life.

How can you do this?

Be kind to yourself and do something nice for yourself – learn some new, fun activity, get a pampering massage done, go for a meal to your favourite restaurant (even if you go alone), go for a long drive away from the city if you enjoy driving, or watch a re-run of your favourite movie. Treat yourself the same way that you would if you were doing it for someone else that you liked a lot. Enjoy the entire experience.

Do something nice for someone else – do random acts of kindness, volunteer at a local charity or just listen to someone who needs to talk without being judged. Being of service without expecting anything in return will make you feel really good.

Be grateful – for all that you have and are surrounded with. If you list each one of your blessings then you will be surprised to know how long the list can be. Try this - Keep a Blessings Jar at home, and every time something nice happens to you, write a small note on a piece of paper, date it, fold it and put it in the Blessings Jar. After a few months or a year, open the jar and read everything – you will feel enormous gratitude for the many blessings that you have had.

Stop comparing yourself to others – each one of us is created to be unique and special in our own way... the way we do things, the principles that we live by, the values that we hold dear and our endeavours. So compare yourself to yourself... how you felt yesterday, the past week, etc., and how you feel today. Send love to yourself... every time you feel a negative thought or feeling about yourself creeping up. Accept your value as a unique person and it will help you feel happier and more confident.

Set small goals – start by setting small realistic goals, achieving them and celebrating the achievement. Slowly move onto setting more challenging goals.

Notice the small pleasurable small stuff around you.

Practice mindful meditation on a regular basis – when we are upset or stressed our breathing becomes quick and shallow, breathing deeply and slowly instantly calms us down mentally and physically.

And remember it is okay to make mistakes and be less than perfect. Just try and be the best version of yourself!

A DEEP, HEAVY WINTER

By Linda M. Crate

depression
is like a deep, heavy winter
full of snow that never
seems to cease or end;
it is numb and quiet reflection
when all you want
is someone to hear you speak -
glittering and sparkling
one may say it's beautiful,
and sometimes life is
even in these darkest moment;
but pretty soon there's dirt in the snow
the sun is swallowed by the clouds
and you are left cold and tired -
there is pain and misery
even anger,
and I try to shovel out and away from this season
but it always has a way of coming back
to swallow away my suns and moons and stars
until I am left in this dark murmur
bereft of anything other than
a silence that isn't golden but rather black and cruel
biting with teeth like those of a vampire
draining me of my energy as it sucks the blood of my soul
out of me,
and some days I can shove the garlic in his mouth and stake him
scattering his ashes before he rises again;
but there are other days where he wins and I succumb to
all the rage and pain
where only sleep can save me from the nightmares.

THE ART OF DEATH

By Ebuwa Ohenhen

We speak of death like it's something simple.
We speak of death like it's easy.
We speak of suicide like it's a walk in the park.

Such arrogance!

Death is an art.
There's an art to taking your own life.

And like all terrible art,
Life is the art you throw in the waste bin.

Death is an art.
If you're going to take your own life,
Then at least go out with a bang,
Let your death be called art.

Death is an art.
It's an art I'm working towards.

This is my suicide poem.

DO NOT MOURN ME.

DAILY REVELATIONS

By Pasithea Chan

Deprived of affection and a sense of belonging
one retires to a sanctuary of isolation.

Arraigned by the acute pain of rejection
the walls become his or her world.

Indicted with selfishness and antisocial behavior
sleep is the best defense and life sentence.

Levied with incessant worries about tomorrow
sense falls to numbness like a baby lulled to sleep.

Yearning for warmth and the need to be heard
one contemplates talking to inanimate objects.

Reprehended for vocalizing one's outlook
of the world, silence becomes the decorum.

Encapsulated with grief, mobility
is running errands for survival only.

Vilified for one's depressive state
smiles are just an anti wrinkle cream.

Engrossed with sadness from one's state
causes palpitation with the slightest change.

Larking with dark thoughts of an early exit
becomes one's favorite pass-time.

Adjourned from engaging in sweet nothings
estranges one around so many happy faces.

Truncated moments of free expression
becomes the only method of communication.

Incapacitated with anger and denial
one falters to bitterness and dismay.

Obliterated from the lives of close ones
confines one to being minuscule.

Neap tide for once is just a moment of rebellion
against reality's gravity pulling one down.

Susceptibility to darkness is a daily revelation
only experienced by ones who face mishaps alone.

Author's Notes: Genre: Acrostic Couplet. This piece is centralized around depression, loneliness, hurt, and emotional demise.

PLEASE STOP
By Cynthia Morrison

Please stop, your parents will miss you,
Please stop before I must hand your mother a tissue,
Please stop, let death be the offender's issue,
Please stop and let your young life continue.

You are not alone with others around,
Seek peace of mind as others have found,
It's not your fault, the trauma and sounds,
Please stop, move forward to gain new ground.

Please stop, you've done nothing wrong,
Please stop, they would only want you to be strong,
Please stop, it is here that you belong,
Please stop, friends and family love you all the days long.

For the suicide victims of the Marjory Stoneman Douglas High School shooting in Parkland, Florida.

CANNULAS
By John Tunaley

One cannula for fluids, one for blood
But none in sight for the soul or spirit;
As a row of guardian trees look down
Into our ward from their winter ridgeline.

It's nearly tea-time but it's 'Nil By Mouth'
For most of us. Lying here prostrated
By the onset of time, fate or self-harm;
The bank-nurses have to hoist our drip feeds.

Down in the tiny chapel there's a box
On the altar to drop in requests for
Prayers; paper pleas for intercession
And angelic hosts to watch over us.
There's no way of washing your soiled hands clean in there.
You must re-join the hospital body for that.

CROW

By Bill Cox

I saw a crow
With a broken wing
Standing by the Highway.
I thought
"I'm like you,
Broken and useless,
Waiting for the end."
When I drove by
The next day,
I saw that crow's remains;
Black feathers,
Blood and bone,
Crushed into the tarmac.
In that moment
As I sped on by
All I felt
Was envy.

GENDERFLUID

By Parvinder Kaur

I'm coughing blood now.
And my dry throat is tired.
Why should I walk a certain way?
Why am I wired?
Why should it matter so much if it is pink that pleases me?
Why is it not acceptable, if a shaven head is what I want to keep?
I fell a million times; you never gave a helping hand.
So why does it bother you, when on high heels, I stand.
Oh! I don't match your choice of clothes? I simply don't want to!
Why should it matter, if it's a dress I elect too?
How is it that the simple language I use seems so incoherent to you?
You and you like million others, shouldn't you be protecting us few?

Don't push us to the ground.
We are not sick.
It is not a phase.
Don't push us to the ground.
A few clouds,
A little piece of the rainbow,
We just want a few warm sun rays.

I CAN FEEL AGAIN NOW THE PILLS ARE OVER

By Ibn Qalam

I can feel again now the pills are over;
I was feeling too much, everything all at once
Like a punch in the jaw that rendered you
Metal dry-mouthed and panicked.

But I can feel again now the pills are over,
And all the tops and bottoms are back.
Where belief comes from above and grief lurks
Below, and three chords draw tears.

And I can feel again now the pills are over,
Panavision's been restored and the mist
Is changing colour, haloed around my love,
And I'm breathless with gratitude.

So, I can feel again now the pills are over,
But cuffs and slights leave bigger bruises
Recompense for broader smiles and renewed
Optimism, if that's not tempting fate?

To see again now the pills are over,
Trying not to regret or rue the lost time
But extend emotion and risk the hurt,
A measured reminder of life for sure.

THE SUICIDE SURROGATE CONFESSES

By LindaAnn LoSchiavo

Perhaps she wished to mimic opera's
Iconic heroines, envisioning
This love as indispensable yet doomed.

Tonight he called, insisting he'll commit
To it. He'll kill himself - he really will.

As usual, she was encouraging.

Then he had second thoughts. He couldn't breathe
The toxic fumes. She might have phoned police
Or notified his family. Instead
She argued with him, "Get back in the truck!"

Obeying her commands, his body wrapped
Around the nameless weight his life became,
Afraid no longer of its siren song.

His absence filled his parents' painbrain, torched
Those memories of suicide attempts.
His girlfriend took his life away from them.

Demanding justice, they watched screens replay
Text messages debating the ideal
Method for meeting death successfully.

"Sorry I let you do this," she confessed.

After the verdict's read, the gavel pounds
The desk for order - and lifts satisfied.

This poem was first published in the spring May 2019 issue of the *Pennsylvania Literary Journal.*

NOTE: The suicide of Conrad Henri Roy III [1995—2014], with encouragement from his long-distance girlfriend, 17-year-old Michelle Carter, was the subject of a noted investigation and involuntary manslaughter trial in Bristol County, Massachusetts, known as the 'texting suicide case.'

THERE ARE BETTER DAYS

By Linda M. Crate

I am not a miserable person
just feel everything deeply and intensely
guess it's the price of feeling,
but I would rather be sensitive in an insensitive world
rather than wrapped in those bones of apathy;
you can have those glittering white fangs
I don't need immortality at that price

sometimes the depression wins,
but sometimes I do
rising on the immortal wings of the phoenix
burning away all this winter and all the vampires too,
until there are no ashes to scatter;
because sometimes the monsters don't win -

there are days I fail,
but I promise myself that there's tomorrow
I will do better then if I find I cannot rise out of the mire;
but sometimes I find that I can fight and when I can
I do -

because I know I am stronger than I sometimes feel
every time I have felt like dying, I lived;
and I have been better for it

so this little light of mine I am going to let it shine
even if some days it is not a glorious and beautiful
sunset, even if some days it's smaller than the light of
a candle; I am going to hold onto this hope
because I am a bird who has been caged too long -
I am going to fly again, and one day
this will all be behind me;
I know there are better days and I will call them by name.

TIGHTROPE

By Hannah Louise MacFarlane

Click your heels three times and hope for the best. I'm walking a tightrope of misdemeanours and a weak heart. When I believed a word they said, I thought for a second that it could be true that perhaps the gentle nature that often won out over the facade of hardness I portrayed would, in any way, shape or form influence good some day. I let that notion stick for far too long within the crevices of my inner most picturesque fallacy and its left marks on the wall that'll sit there until the whole thing falls down.

It's not got long, either. The prima ballerina in my mind is doing pirouettes around memories and her pointe is not strong enough to save herself from falling more than once. Each time she lets her heel touch the ground it wrecks another portrait of what I thought happy felt like or what it meant and now it looks like a jigsaw puzzle with missing pieces and nobody in the world seems to care as much as I do about the empty spaces.

I am the empty space, I think. I am the empty void that is overflowing with fountains of well-wishes and promises of what could have been and should have been but I am an empty space that is being designed into a graveyard. Inside hope finds its final resting place and I think the new world order will be aligned when finally I succumb to the mass and accept I belong there too. I am the lesson that they teach about could have been but will never be, and everyone has something to learn from.

Lessons are lesions, mostly. Grooves carved into my mind, which in turn corpse themselves into four major categories; pain, loneliness, grief and false hope. The last is the most lethal of all because the proceeding leave no room for question but the last? The last allows for slips in the armour and the infection to spread from the mind to the heart and no amount of Ibuprofen can cure that. All you can do is restore factory settings and try again but it'll never feel new again.

The stage is set, the top offenders have front row seats. That prima ballerina is still fumbling through the wreckage and salvaging nothing from the warfare. It's just a matter of time before the show is over, before the dust settles and the hecklers come rolling in uninvited in their various hues of desperation and brutal honestly. The crowd are placing bets on if she'll have a final bow. It doesn't look likely this time.

SCARS

(noun: straight lines and curves around ruthless stories)
By Parvinder Kaur

Hi D!

I don't remember the last time we exchanged e-mails. It's been long. Haha! Remember how we checked up on each other every day? I really hope you do. We ranted and wrote long paragraphs on some days. And on the others it was just a semicolon. The first time, I didn't know what it meant. It was so confusing. But you wrote back pretty quick. You said it can be used when you want to end a sentence, but continue it anyway.

It is weird. You have just stopped sending e-mails. It has been 21 days since you last wrote. However, I did not break my promise. Not yet. But I feel tired today. I don't think I will write from tomorrow.

I told you this a few days back. I was annoyed at something. And I hadn't made the promise of the day, because there was no e-mail from you. So I dug out the blade from the back yard. I had buried and hidden it so well. It took me forever to find it. The scars from that day were deeper and wider than they seemed to be. The blade was rusted and I think the wounds are infected now. It hurts too much. I can't tell anyone about it. I am too scared. maybe mum noticed me walking differently. But no questions asked.

It is too hot outside. So, wearing shorts or frocks is risky. I wish you'd tell me what to do. Why don't you text back? A semicolon will do. I hope, you not replying has nothing to do with the last email you sent. It was just a full stop. I think your finger accidentally hit that button. You always had silly errors in your e-mail. I know this one was an error too. Wasn't it? It did not mean anything else right? Answer me please! I's so tired of asking you the same question every day. Why won't you just answer me? Just send a semicolon please. I did everything you asked me to do. I threw my blades away. I went to the beach that day. I've started eating ice cream. I folded all my clothes and I've started to keep my room clean. I've done everything. EVERYTHING!

I am tired now. I really want to sleep. It is tough to fall asleep. I saw this article on the internet the other day. About a medicine. I think you told me about it once. You said if I took a tablet, I'd fall asleep easily. I'll take a few. I really want it to work. I hope I get to see you whenever I wake up.

Take care until then alright? I miss you. Come and check on me soon.

Good night D.
(P.S. I wish you had told me your name.)

Best,

Me

RESOLVE
By Barbara Hawthorn

I will do it
  don't think I wouldn't
    just because I've been here before
      that was then
        there were reasons I stayed

exit plans were just delayed
  never
    shelved
always that loop that plays inside my head
  that nagging voice
    … better off dead…

time
  finally
    to slam the door
     do a bolt

face it
  I'm useless
    just a waste of space
      the tank is empty
       and now is now

So this is goodbye
  this time for real
    when you get this letter
      assume I'm done

oh, and PS
  tell Mum I love her
    none of this is her fault

THE DAY I DIED
By Katrina Cattermole

I was young I was a fool
I caused you heartache
How could I be so cruel

You said you were in a barn
You were about to take your life
You were all alone with the rope to fasten around your neck
I was a fool
I caused you heartache
How could you be so cruel

Lets talk
Come to me please, lets talk I said
We talked
We cried
We hugged
We loved again
We were both fools

You caused me such pain
It was me or her
You wanted us both
Then you choose her
So I lost my way
I lost everything I knew
I lived for you and you threw it away
I have no life without you
I wanted to die
I told you so
Thoughts of me dead did not deter you from your new love
You held on tight but I kept up the fight
I had to keep going but I was already dead
I died that day

The monster I choose took my life and soul
The mind games, the abuse, the torture and rapes
Killed every part of my being
My mind was being destroyed
I could not escape
I had nowhere to hide
Oh how I tried, so hard to be free

Was this my life now
It had to be

I asked for help, no one could hear me
My pleas unnoticed
Get over it
Move on
Leave him
You will be fine

Oh how I tried.
I had to get out
I had to be free
I was trapped

Use a knife, use the meds, use the vodka, or a gun?
The blade felt good that I ran across my arms
Watching the crimson red blood flow and drip into my palm
on the floor was the best and brightly shone
The pain is still there
But not from the cuts
It comes from within
And the damage inside

He killed me the day he took my soul
Who cares anyway?
Not me

I choose the knife he forced me too
The devil sharpened it well
Swish swish swish swish like his tail
Smirk on his face looking down at me
With glistening eyes wide, jaws clenched with hunger
Kill yourself girl he said very calm
So I chopped with pure hatred and misery
Curled in the corner covered in my life's blood
Was this now the blood of the devil I think?
I cried with no pain only pure self-loathing
He made me a nothing
How can this be

So each day he gave me head-fuck and pain
I get out the knife
It's the devil inside me now,
Pours out and wipes away

The scars tell my tale that he did to me
I feel ashamed and hide it well
Who cares
Not me

I broke free from that monster who controlled my life
Then answered my phone
Coughing and choking
He said please come to me

Lights from my car were shining on his
mid nowhere in the darkest of night
I went to the field with my mate
Found him slumped in his car, engine still running
The smell of fumes was retching for me
Yet he was in there,
Oh God he was in there
Let me get him out
Panic set in I couldn't breathe
I pulled him and he fell to wet grass
He said hysterically
You will never stay with me

The ambulance came
and policemen too
Found the axe he was going to use
I could have been dead too, but my mate was there
But he survived, it was all a game to him
So be it this time but there were many more
Reality does not kick in, but its pure mind shit

Many times he wrote letters to say goodbye
I was frantic and checked on him each time
I still feel the knot in my belly
I could not bare the thought
How could I live with it if he was dead

Oh no no no
Eeach time it was a game
A controlling game
Next time I will let him get on with it
Yea we will see
So now I'm crazy
I cut myself
I want to die

My mind is stuck and cant get out
I look at Google and ways to die
No pain no pain no pain
Quick quick quick
No suffer no suffer no suffer

Then I stop as if nothing is wrong
Because I can't do that
The click in my head says stop it
You can't do it
I have kids
I have a dog
But the pain inside is so strong
I don't want to be here
To see the autumn leaves on the trees
The spring flowers
The shimmering sun
Or the glare of the snow
I'm trapped in this nightmare 24/7
My mind doesn't stop thinking of all the trauma
Why am I here
Why
What is the point
I cant stop thinking
God damn it

Now you won't speak
Now you won't talk
Now you don't acknowledge me at all.
I gave you children
I gave you everything you wanted
And more
This kills me inside
I don't need to kill myself
I'm already dead

Interview with Katrina

What motivated you to write your piece Katrina?

Well, I'm a 53 year old woman who had a good childhood and terrific married life up until when my mother became terminally ill in 2012. I was happily married to my childhood sweetheart whom I'd met when I was 14 and he 15. We had motorbikes, sports cars, horses, dogs, a house, holidays and lots of fun and laughter. Obviously we all have our up and downs in any relationship, but we were looking forward for our future together. And then my mum died and I lost my way.

Can you explain this a little more?

Well, I went into depression from the grief and, at the same time, had severe menopausal symptoms. During that time I went to a school reunion and met someone who at first was just a friend and we connected and chatted on Facebook, but soon he started playing mind games with me, and started controlling my life. In the ensuing mayhem my husband no longer recognised me, and found another woman to love. I was devastated and confused, I got into a relationship with this person and it all became unbelievably crazy. I became isolated and alone and really didn't understand what was happening. It became a very toxic relationship, with physical and psychological abuse, rape and punishment in all forms if I were to even mention my husband's name or other friends. All I ever wanted was my husband to come back to me and save me, but he had gone for good. I tried to escape on my own several times but it was impossible. He destroyed my mind. Finally I broke free, but I now live day to day with C-PTSD, no friends, isolation, and no trust in anyone. The day I lost my gorgeous husband was *The Day I Died.*

And is that why you wrote it?

Yes, I wrote it because I am still suffering day to day with what happened and thought it may help to release some of my trauma and heal some of my pain. Everything still haunts me, including my suicide attempts and self-harming; mental abuse is far worse than physical abuse and carries no visible scars.

Can you give me just one incident of his mental abuse that had caused you so much trauma?

My perpetrator played so many games with me, and if he didn't get his own way he would threaten to kill himself. For example, once he called me and told me his was in his car and was going to kill himself, and lured me to a field in Suffolk in the middle of the night to save him. I found him in his car, with a pipe from the exhaust through the window, which was stuffed with blankets. The ambulance was called along with the police, but he just made a mockery out of it all by saying he wasn't really going to finish himself off. I was absolutely in turmoil and couldn't get my head around any of it, it was so extreme and cruel. Another time he wanted to do a double suicide with me and taunted me with it all the time as I always said no. He called me a chicken. Another time he sharpened a knife, gave it to me, and told me to kill myself whilst he went to bed. My husband was my everything and now I had a monster who would not leave me alone. It was all my fault, I deserved it. I loathed myself.

How did you manage to handle these emotions and experiences?

I didn't really manage to handle my emotions because they were total chaos. One minute I was up the next he would bring me down. When I told my husband I wanted to die and I needed help, he wouldn't help. I didn't understand how he would rather let his two children be motherless than help me get away from this perpetrator.

What happened when you finally got away?

I had no friends so got so lonely that I started to befriended 'heavy' people. They either wanted sex, I would run, they would want to rape me, never succeeded, or they would want money or a roof over their head. So eventually I learned to hold everything in from people because they didn't want to know, or to help, or to care or to understand. I isolated myself even more. I couldn't sleep, I couldn't eat, I couldn't function. I did have one male friend who would talk to me, but he was a very troubled person himself and ended up drinking himself to death. I was devastated and wanted to end my life with him. I soldiered on though, with more grief, self-harming, hitting the bottle and having very suicidal thoughts but keeping everything to myself. Not pleasant.

How did you managed to move past everything to where you are today?

I haven't really moved on or away from these thoughts. I have just deviated, hoping that one day something will be good in my life again, something to lift me up and away from it all. I am still trapped in the nightmare, and have feelings of despair. I try to do little things, but motivation and self hatred stops me from doing what I really want to achieve. I used to be bubbly, lots of things to do, laughter and lots to look forward too. Happiness and contentment. Now I am not even a shadow of myself. I was once told I will never be who I was. I agree with that statement now. I was aghast when I was first told but it's true, I will never be who I was. So I have had to accept it. Like I have accepted everything that happened.

What does the future hold?

Personally had never felt suicidal or self harmed before this started and now I wake up every day wishing I didn't wake up at all. At the moment I don't see any future, if I did it would all go wrong anyway. I have no purpose anymore. Having a purpose would be great. I need to grieve for my mother properly, and grieve for my marriage and ex husband, to which I never had the chance. A quote from Shakespeare "I think the devil will not have me damned lest the oil that's in me should set hell on fire."

I will find my way though, I have been to the most darkest of places and survived. I will survive. I do not give up easily and even though I fail now, I will get right back up and try again. I am not crazy, I am not a fool; I am me. And me is broken at the moment, but I will be back. A different me, apparently, but I will be back.

Any advice for anyone else facing their own troubles and trauma?

Firstly I don't want to be hypocrite and say there is light at the end of the tunnel straight-away. I guess there is for some, but I personally have not found the source of that light yet and when I do see a glimmer of light, it is instantly put out. But I am learning to love myself again, whoever I may be. All I can say is if you feel suicidal, that moment doesn't normally last longer than an hour or so, so hold on, and remember the thought will go soon, keep fighting. Do it for you. No one else. YOU. There is a massive stigma with mental health and it needs to be addressed. It does not mean you are mad or crazy or insane. Absolutely anyone can get depression, anxiety, panic, suicidal thoughts or self-harm. There is help out there, so don't ever be afraid to speak out and tell other people how you feel.

THE CALL OF THE SEA

By Mary Anne Zammit

My heart is empty.
My thoughts are black.
But the sea calls out my name, calls me to do it.
To put an end to this nightmare.
I stand on the boat, heading towards an unknown destination.

It is hard when no one loves you.
When no one looks at the sea with your eyes.
And instead you become an object of someone 's desire.

So I go towards the edge of the boat.
It is time to go.
'Come on, be strong.'
I jump into sea.

Memories come and take me back to the village surrounded by fields.
I am working my family in Africa.
I dreamt of leaving my country and starting a new life, away from
war.
I dreamt of him holding my hands.
He promised to take me to a new land.
I followed him.
To the stars and moon.
Instead, he sold me to other men.
Heavy rain on my lids.

I am sinking into waters.
If I scream no one will hear my cries.
Only the sea.
Death has come, I wanted it, I willed it.
I once had a dream.

Now the sea has taken it all.

FLAT DISTORTIONS

By John Tunaley
*Inspired by Francesca Woodman Photograph Exhibition, Tate,
Liverpool.*

In an abandoned spaghetti factory,
Her nude body; obscured by doors, flattened
By panes of glass, distorted by mirrors;
Is hung by the hair from a clothes-hook.

A shedding skin of peeling wallpaper
Partially hides the clothes-pegs clipped to her
Smudged nipples. By the end, she'd forgotten
How to read music; could no longer play.

Instead she concentrated on making
Silver-gelatine prints of a coiled eel rising
From a pot beside her fogged bare torso...

All those exposed, blurred selves ...her as
Naked angel... as crucified hanging Christ...
As suicide by jumping, aged twenty-two...

NOTE: Francesca Stern Woodman (April 3, 1958 – January 19, 1981) was an American photographer
best known for her black and white pictures featuring either herself or female models. Her work
continues to be the subject of much critical acclaim and attention, years after she died by suicide at the
age of 22, in 1981.

INTO NO MAN'S LAND (OF WW1)

By Cynthia Morrison

Don't go out there or I'll tell your Mother,
I'd much rather swill a dram if I had my druthers,
"That was a bastard flying pig," as they felt the shutter,
Soldiers know the sound all too well, as does no other.

Here comes one now, a hissing Jennie,
For every one of those I wish I had a Yank's penny,
Where's your gas mask? You heard Sergeant McKinney,
Trust me lad, your days shall be plenty.

A tear in his eye and look of disbelief,
I reached to offer him some of my bully beef,
"I'm going" he said "I've had enough of this grief,"
"Stay right here lad I'm going to fetch some relief."

Upon my return the young lad was gone,
I think his name was Thomas, no maybe it was John,
His rifle lay down with bayonet un-drawn,
The hellish sounds of the frightful night reached out to greet the dawn.

A short desperate letter I found near his dirty knapsack,
"Forgive me everyone, as I write this in near pitch black,
No longer shall I exist, leaving all as I enter into merciless attack,
I go to seek an eternal peace, let this be on the enemy's back."

Prisoners of war pulled him from the barbed wire,
Uniform torn and scorched under fire,
There he rests, facing skyward under the mire,
Lying deeper now than the trench and all its hellfire.

I WILL NOT SUCCUMB

By Heera Nawaz

Though the odds are stacked irrevocably against solitary me,
I vow to never succumb nor give in nor give up.
For those facing tyranny and not expressing it,
are equivalent of emptying God's ever replenishing cup.

I will fight back for I am in the pangs of hurtful pain.
Trying my utmost to grasp for air and definitely not succumb,
for I am indeed made of stronger and sterner stuff,
willing to sweat it out until my bones are numb.
Indeed, life is not fair when the means are foul,
to uproot an innocent soul who will falter and fall,
so, I should courageously and resolutely spring forth,
and stand proud, resolute and tall.

Society can prick me with its unceremonious threats and barbs,
to make even a conscientious person like me lose hope and heart.
So, I felt enthused to harken myself to God's clarion call,
and know that He will help me when things fall apart.

For God is great, I know in my bones that He will save me,
and give me the requisite fortitude to face formidable foes,
as I know he will heal my crushed, broken semblance of a soul,
and help me eliminate my every increasing worries and woes.

Indeed, they excel in torturing, tormenting and chastising my soul,
for which I should not relent, but remain vociferous and strong,
for I know I have the power of sacred and benign forgiving,
which enables me to eke out goodness even from their wrong.

Interview with Heera

Why did you write your poem Heera?

In life, there are two types of thoughts that can course through one's mind: positive thoughts and negative thoughts. It has been proved that one attracts the kind and genre of thoughts that one already has in one's mind; like a magnet attracting nails. So, if one is sanguine and optimistic, one will readily see that one attracts a beautiful kaleidoscope of positive feelings and emotions. The same applies to negative thoughts where, if one has a negative attitude, one will attract even more negativity. So, one should try to school one's self to be positive, which is not something which is very easy to do, but something which is definitely worth the effort.

I was going through a bad patch, a riveting lean phase in my life, where my friendships were not fructifying into beautiful liaisons but instead were becoming ones inundated with lies, cheating and malpractices. I was getting pretty het-up and frustrated, and both my friends and enemies were having a field day at my expense. Things reached a head. I decided to take a break, review my plans and dreams and rid myself of all the toxic people in my life.

I wrote the poem and decided to stick it in my cupboard and glance at it every time I needed a boost, a fill-up and a surge of confidence and positive thinking. Indeed, it has been a very powerful indicator, and I would like those who are feeling low or forlorn to read this poem and poems like this to rejuvenate, refurbish and refresh one's mind to go out there and fight it out, fair and square, using prayers and meditations as one's 'weapons.' One should summon enough determination and courage to take a leap of faith, fight and destroy one's negative thoughts and reach the goal of positive beautiful dreams and aspirations.

SUICIDE (SOME REASONS OF COMMITTING SUICIDE)

By Maliha Hassan

Plundering, killing, committing crime,
All sorts of evil deeds in his prime time.
Caught and cornered, could see his doom,
No escape to be found, no repentance no room.
Finally hung himself behind the bars,
Silently, stealthily in the wee hours.
Became a victim of his own doings,
To set an example for human beings.

Forced against his wishes to be married
Intended to study not ready to be carried.
Pleaded, cried and longed to be heard,
To carry out mission, as freely as a bird.
To live for a cause, work hard for gain,
Toil day and night, cannot restrain.
Too weak to fight the opposing forces,
Useless to convince dominant faces.

No wishes fulfilled creating self-hate.
No patience, no tolerance, no time to wait.
Impatiently waiting for the opening of gate.
For opportunities to come, should not be late.
Mercilessly takes his life, was in such a haste.
Thinks waiting in life is a sheer waste.
Notes down his message to tell a tale,
For all and sundry who therefore wail.

Due to poverty could not meet his ends,
Many mouths to feed, and affairs to tend.
His starving children could no longer bear,
The falling health, consequences clear.
The crying kids just a morsel do crave,
Makes a bold decision to consign to waves.
Settling in the depth to meet their fate.
Ends mercilessly to show mirror to the state.

Jealousy not gone, envy so pressed upon,
Unable to grip and catch by the horn.
Falls into depression and anxiety,

Lacks faith in Allah Almighty.
Parents, siblings, friends sure to be blamed,
Attitude, mood and behaviour when not the same.
Be cautious and observant, rush for a cure,
Symptoms such seen, then why to ignore?

LISTEN, DON'T SPEAK

By Linda M. Crate

I remember when you made that joke
about suicide
even when I begged you not to,
and was that joke about a man hanging himself
really so funny that you had to tell it?
when I told you that my uncle had hung himself
you weren't apologetic, at all,
but rather defensive insisting that you didn't
know him;
but you did know that I asked you to stop
when I saw the direction the joke would go
I will never fathom why you had to be so cruel -
you made me feel small and voiceless
as all the other people who talked over and around me
like my voice and my opinions were null and void
simply because you wouldn't hear me,
and it made me angry;
because we are always told that our voice matters
yet there are some who choose to refuse to listen -
maybe if people took more time to listen than to speak
there would be less people who locked themselves
up so tight inside that they felt that death
was the only option to save themselves.

SAY IT

By Guy Morris

It's not often heard in modern day life,
between boyfriend, girlfriend, husband and wife.
We get too complacent, always in a hurry,
we often forget, but seem not to worry.
SAY IT, to your loved ones, for those whom you care,
before its too late a they're no longer there.
SAY IT and mean it to all whom you love,
and may God smile upon you from heaven above.
SAY IT right now and bear no regret,
it may be the last chance that you ever get.
Of what am I speaking?
Why? Have you no clue?
It's those three little words that say...

I
LOVE
YOU!

RESCUE

By Bill Cox

"Pull yourself together"
That's what I was told,
Put your brave face on,
Carry on down the road.

But when life got crazy
And the pressure piled on
I felt myself shatter,
All hope and joy were gone.

With nowhere left to turn
I contemplated the worst,
I felt myself go under,
In despair I was submersed.

My story didn't end there though,
A friend offered their hand.
Grasping tight I was heaved up
Now on solid ground I stand.

That person rescued me
Through sympathy and care.
Will you do likewise
When a friend needs you there?

Life is hard, at times a struggle,
Care can drag us down,
But if we look out for each other,
Then none of us will drown.

ON A SUNDAY
By David Lohrey

The man killed himself on a Sunday.
On a Sunday!
Why not wait?
Why couldn't he wait until Monday,
for a time when suicide is more appropriate?
For a time when many others
feel like ending their lives.

Sunday! The day of coloured eggs
and little girls in patent leather
is no time to do oneself in. Sunday
is a day for French toast and chicken dinner.
It's the day families gather for biscuits
and gravy, and second helpings.
It's the only day Uncle Billy can sleep in.
It's a day for singing.

If you are going to kill yourself,
why not do it on Saturday afternoon?
The day teenage girls wait to be
taken out by handsome boys.
There is a weekend ritual: screwing
in the back-seat of the Chevrolet,
hanging out, drinking strawberry shakes,
and, if one is lucky, tasting nookie.

Suicide may have the ring of truth,
but it's nothing more than an act
of vulgar desperation. It belongs
to a night of vomit, not to the morning
after. It has nothing to do with choir.
It has nothing to say to joy. Sundays are
the negation of self-doubt; Sunday
is a day for delightful worship.

Where did he do it? And how? I'm only curious.
Did he run into a brick wall? On a Sunday
there's nothing on TV; now that's a good reason
to blow one's brains out. Or maybe the griddle
cakes burned. The maid was late and forgot
to make orange juice. The matinee was sold out.

He got to the carving station and found the prime
rib was bloody.
There's a pimple on his sweet ass.
His bank account was frozen.
The car wouldn't start. When you
are suicidal, any reason will do, trust
me. I've killed myself many times over.
I killed myself just yesterday,
because my shoe lace broke.
Don't tell me he had no reason.

He couldn't decide, that's why. He killed
himself out of spite. He'd made a pact.
He promised to be home for supper. He agreed
to end it all when he heard women can't vote
in Argentina. He read last night in the New York Times
that people eat baby goats in Transylvania.
He couldn't accept the fact that people in Japan
sleep in their pyjamas.

The world is nothing but injustice. His favourite show
was cancelled when its star got pregnant. His
neighbour's dachshund, Speedy, was hit by a car.
He chose Sunday morning to get back at his mother.
She overcooks his eggs which he prefers sunny side up.
She serves them on the floor with too much ketchup.
She told him there was no more coffee;
he'd have to drink tea. He hated his father, too.

Sunday is as good a day as any.
This is how atheists think.
They break into churches and
shit on the pews. They are heartless.
My best friend Carrie was attacked
for holding hands with a white girl.
And you wonder why he killed himself on Sunday?
I'm surprised he didn't kill himself every day of the week.

SUDDENLY AT HOME

By Trisha Lawty

A cup of tea.
Warm, sweet tea,and I need warmth and sweetness.
Fill the kettle, think only of filling the kettle.
Filling the kettle makes sense,
when nothing else in this world makes sense.
What next?
Fill the teapot.
Tea bags and boiling water.
Brewing warm sweet tea makes sense,
when nothing else in my world makes sense
I do need warmth and sweetness.
Drinking warm, sweet tea gives me normality,
When nothing in my life is normal.

DYING

By Robin Barratt

I sit silently, hands by my side, my eyes closed.
I can hear the faint sounds of the cars on the road in the distance,
and youths chatting as they pass on the path nearby.
I hear birds in the tress,
a bee humming,
a dog barking,
a siren in the distance.

I feel tired, so tired.
This life has drained me,
taken everything from me.
This bleak, dark world has destroyed my soul, my being.
It has taken everything from me.
Everything.

I once had a good life,
a job I loved,
a house that was home,
a wife I adored.

I laughed and joked and loved,
and even once danced naked in the rain.

But now I have nothing.
I have no one.
I am alone.

Tears slide slowly down my cheeks,
as I breathe deeply and open my eyes and look up.
I want to see the blue sky one last time.
So beautiful, so clear, so crisp, so clean.

I close my eyes again and let the darkness take me,
as blood drops silently into the growing pool of red on the floor.

I'm finally free.

Published in *Naked in the Rain* by Robin Barratt.

THOSE LEFT BEHIND
By Donna Zephrine

Suicide does not just cause pain to those who harm themselves.
The hurt spreads to the whole family.
Family members might try to reach out, want to help, but maybe
don't know how.
Impossible to know the right thing to say or do.
The person might push you away, become violent, or isolate and
withdraw.
They may turn to drugs or alcohol to cope with their feelings.
Little do they realize the drugs add to their problems and sadness.
How do you help someone who doesn't want your help?
Many families don't understand mental illness.
They may not know how severe things are getting.
There may even be signs like superficial cutting, past attempts, or
there could be no signs at all.
Impossible to know what is going on in their head.
If they do not want you to know, you won't.
Families feel helpless.
And then one day it might be too late.
They find their loved one dead by their own doing.
How can the human brain comprehend something so painful and
complicated?
Why? Why go this far? Why not let me help? What could I have done?
What were they thinking?
The survivor's guilt starts to kick in.
Why am I still here if they are not?
A parent who loses their child somehow has to go on outliving their
child.
There is no closure.
Some use religion to try to reason with suicide. Maybe it was a
demon, the devil? Anything to try and make sense of the
unimaginable.
Those who loved a person who committed suicide are left to try and
pick up the pieces event though the puzzle is shattered into a million
pieces.

ONE ALMOST FLEW OVER THE CUCKOO'S NEST

By Sara Spivey

I awoke in confusion, head and body feeling heavy, drugged even. No recollection of where I was, or how I got there.

I was in a bed – clothes on, my hand searched around instinctively for my bag, my belongings. Yes they were there on the bed with me. An eerie silence surrounded me, whilst my sensations tried desperately to clamber back into my realm of consciousness. A pricking of a memory forming.

Noise, people shopping, dizzy, falling down... then the hospital. A vague visual of a doctor talking to me, problems with the language barrier. More confusion. Then a little comprehension. The doctor said I had collapsed, taken pills and was unhappy and suggested an overnight stay in the hospital. Sounded weird but kind. I remember thinking this was reasonable, however, given how I was feeling at the time. I had agreed. Wrong decision! Lack of understanding between two languages equals chaos and mayhem.

Trying with great effort to assemble myself as best I could, I slowly stood up, wobbled, steadied myself on the bed with wheels {a vague recollection of having being moved during the night}, no shoes on, just my socks. Odd.

Slowly, shakily I made my way along the empty, white, sterile corridor trying to make sense of my situation and find someone to help me. It was all so silent and abandoned. Then suddenly a middle aged man, in a terrible state appeared around the corner, scaring me half to death. He looked vacant and dirty, his movements reminding me of Frankenstein. I feebly smiled, no response or recognition, just a vacant, dead stare back.

I continued. I came across a large living area, one side furnished with a line of plastic chairs in primary colours, the other side, a long, plastic, white table with plastic white chairs, a few cushions, a TV high up on the wall and nothing else. Dawning was rising that this was not an ordinary hospital ward.

My displacement was interrupted by three, maybe teenagers, or twenty-somethings, all seeming to know one another. The girl caught my attention. She looked so fragile, tiny fairy like figure, milky complexion except for the delicate purple rings around her eyes, from tiredness, sadness or drugs maybe? She seemed to be oblivious to everyone and appeared to be floating around on her stockinged tiptoes, humming gently and observing the minimal objects in the room with incredible interest. She spoke occasionally to the two males but I had no idea what they were saying. She actually appeared happy in her solitary bubble but also required numerous hugs from her two friends. This was the moment that the first emotion started to jerk within, worry. Was this what I thought it was?

As I walked nervously back into the corridor to search the other way, an orderly, literally holding up a man who could barely function, making strange sounds with his mouth hanging open, the penny finally dropped! I asked the orderly for help. All he said was the doctor would be along soon.

I carried on, anxiety building, I couldn't find a door even. I hadn't eaten in hours {when it did arrive, that was also served in plastic containers and was the main event}, and I needed the toilet. At last, I was shown a room with two very sad, older looking women just sitting on their respective beds, motionless. The look of downtrodden mouths and an overwhelming feeling of hopelessness was virtually tangible in that room. They had been here awhile it would seem, their moisturisers, shampoos, toothbrushes were all neatly set up in their shared bathroom. Not a word was uttered, like it was too much effort even to speak or attempt a smile. I shuddered as I left the room.

I demanded a doctor now. 'Soon they will be here.' I simply had to wait, besides, I still felt heavy and tired and knew I had to get my thoughts together, and quickly.

At about 10am two men, the doctors, came by and asked how I was, in English, which was a relief.

'Great, I feel good, when can I go?'

'You can't,' was the unbelievable reply'. The paralysis of fear was taking hold, prickling sensations running up and down my arms, cold and clammy hands.

'What do you mean? I have to be at work this afternoon.' I asked for water, my throat had become terribly dry now.

'Do you know where you are Miss?'

'No, not exactly.'

'The psychiatric ward and we believe you are unsafe to leave!'

'What? I'm sorry, I thought I was just staying overnight to rest and then go. I have been generally unwell but not of a mental nature.'

'Sorry, you're staying for now,' and then they were gone... That was my 4 minute diagnosis? I was nothing like the others here. It was a mistake!

I went straight into panic mode; my god what if I'm imprisoned here for years? What if I get locked in and no-one knows and the stream of relentless, negative horrors continued on a Halloween carousel.

First call, my mother, my friends. Explain. Their shock was

palpable too. I persuaded my mother to talk directly to the doctor – he said the same. The phone was returned to me and the last words I heard my mother say was; 'I promise you, I promise you, I will get you out of there, OK?' I replied okay, dubiously and slowly, quietly lay back down on the bed on my left side, knees tucked into my chest and a wash of loneliness, helplessness and fear took hold which silently worked its way through my mind and body over and over. I was totally isolated in a place I shouldn't be through lack of understanding, and if I made a fuss it would make it worse.

After 30 minutes or so, although it felt like an eternity, I tried to form some kind of action plan. I sought out the doctors again, tried to explain that the drugs I was talking about were too many prescription medications that I had been issued and were creating these bad symptoms. My mother got on the phone again and said she would fly out and get me if necessary, as I was meant to be leaving for London in two days, where my own doctors could take care of me.

At last it worked; they agreed to let me go, if I signed a self-release form so they were not responsible. Cool. 'Just get me the hell out of here!'

After a day, on reflection I couldn't help feeling a connection, a pity, an awful waste of existence for each individual I had bumped into. I was one of the lucky ones. These extremely unhappy individuals, perhaps suicide on their mind, loss of mind, control, senses, whatever, were there for their own - and possibly others' - protection. The other way of looking at it however, was they were both prisoners of their own conditions and minds, and the restraints put upon them by either and/or the hospital or relatives.

Anyone considering that their life's not so sunny should seriously have a couple of days in a similar ward; it would definitely change your outlook on life for the better. Freedom is an outstanding gift!

FAREWELL RED
By Barbara Hawthorn

his outrageous furnace blast of hair
          will never have a grey thread
                    dead is so   irrevocably dead
has his mother snipped a fiery curl or two to keep?
          something to weep over?
                    Keepsake   heart ache   heartbreak?

she looked as though she had no tears left
          drained   utterly bereft and bleak
all those inevitable could-should-if only-might have been
          ominous background drum beat
                    pounding like a migraine

he left no note as such - nothing special for his mum
          they found his journal
                    intended surely solely for his eyes?
a different man from the one we saw
          he dwelt in a world filled with S H I T
                    said it in capitals   again and again
          all our foolish lives so full of C R A P
                    jolts of language   blunt and raw
was the jovial uncle act just a part he played?

at the funeral a photo montage   power point presentation
          looped silently on the wall throughout
goofy kid... thrill seeker... risky reckless sports
                    speed... petrol fumes... and noise
it didn't seem so dull
          those bright days   caught on family film
but nobody it seems records the dead of night
          there behind the fun-fury façade
                    lurked desperation and stress unvoiced
his mates bemused   in shock
          agony to watch them try to speak
                    the speeches they'd prepared all week
                              they looked in such rude health themselves
as only well-grounded thirty-somethings can

out of our depth too   us older ones   uncles and aunts
          too awkward to ask how he did it
                    dead is dead   and no-one said

we just remembered him   the boisterous kid
        recalled how we tied everything down
                prepared for trouble
                        sticking plaster   standing by
when the red headed trio came to visit
        seething with pent-up energy   a few volts short of hysteria

his brothers   shadowed with sadness   bewildered
        cling to their wives   will go on
                I dare say   to live out their lives
sober men
        year after year...
                ...day after fruitful day
                        their flaming hair inevitably turning grey

UNDERTOW

By Hannah Louise MacFarlane

She held the hand she kissed ever so gently as the blood pumped around my veins and sank my heart into motion faster than any grand prix I have ever known to exist. The sea air filled my lungs with a triumphant exclamation that not all air was created equal; a soaring reminder that this air was better than the rest, cadenced in a solemn chill to reprimand the years since I had allowed it to sustain me. The ground was tougher to walk on than I remembered, but I couldn't tell if I had the sand or the weakness in my knees to thank for that. In flashes I remembered the ease of running for hours, wind in my hair, no care in the world as my sister splashed in the waves and we squealed at the icy blue and pretended we were grown-ups, making margaritas out of fruit punch and using straws as cigars. We were a restless sort of youth, the kind that formed clubs and learned leadership from facilitating games of tag and how to bend and break rules with the notion of sunset versus street-lamp and what time we were to report back to our mother's for dinner. We used hoodies for goalposts and still wondered why our backs were covered in sand, or why we couldn't chase the tide to retrieve the fifteenth ball that had been kicked in the fathoms below that summer. The air filled my lungs with its very own poison yet reached my soul in places that had been hard to find without a prescription and a razor blade for a very long time.

I thought of that version of me, the young girl in my memory. She had no idea what harrowing tales awaited her future, she had no idea the mountains she had yet to climb and the forces that would beckon the worst kind of demons to strip the light from her eyes. She was worthy of so much but it would take years for her to ever come to understand that bizarre phenomenon. She still doesn't quite understand it. She still shudders when hands come into contact with her skin and tenses up when someone looks at her for too long. Her head turns every time a new face enters a crowded room and she cowers her gaze as she enters a crowd, scanning it like a little girl checking for monsters under her bed. She had no idea that one day the sandcastles she built would turn into fortresses, steadily guarding her nimble soul from turmoil and disconnect. I thought of the adventures that little girl had taken throughout her life to get to where she was now, hair blowing in that crisp wind and her jaw trembling in fear despite the absence of a real threat. The threat lived inside her skin, each cell bestowing a different memory. The cells on her arms riddled in restraint, the cells on her hips holding harsh fingernails dipped into flesh, the cells on her eye socket a walk-in wardrobe of palms, fists, cold floors and blurred vision. Now here back in this place that was so ripe with the trauma the tide hadn't washed away.

I watched the waves crash against the cliff edge, the one I would climb up and scramble down before the waters blocked off my escape to safety. I would sit there for hours and write my stories, sing handwritten songs, and plan a future that looked a lot happier than the reality of the cards I was dealt. My fingers curled and dug into the flesh of my palms as I recalled the first time he climbed up to meet me and showed an interest in the stories I was writing. Barely a teen, far from a woman, and he steadfast turned me into a compilation of survivors guilt and a bountiful load of self hatred that the razor blade could not cut away, so with each horizontal tear in my flesh I wished for a death that I felt so deserving of I could taste it as the water of my bathtub turned pink at age thirteen. Age fourteen it was a deep red. Age fifteen I'd lost more weight that I had left on my body and the only closed doors that were allowed within my world were those of hospital rooms and classrooms. That was on the days I was able to get out of bed long enough to see the inside of one of those. He took my favourite air and turned it into a noose that took all the air out of every room I have ever walked in.

Then I was on the beach with her. She held the hand she kissed and she whispered how green my eyes were. She told me the things she loved about my smile and the dimple on my cheek. How she loved the life we were living together. The flashes of his claws scratching my hopes and dreams away were replaced with the smell of hand sanitizer from hospital wards and the scars on my wrist that have turned white itched as I remembered the feeling of the needle sewing my wounds shut. I looked around a world that I loved for so long and suffocated in the pain, the grief and the longing for death that had replaced any feelings of tenderness – and then she kissed me. I stopped breathing my own air for a single second and breathed her in, bringing me back to the then and there. That wasn't my world anymore.

This was a world we shared. Our world is not darkened by black dogs or wounds that never heal. Our world spins a little slower when we are together and comprises of my stomach hurting because of intense laughter, not pain. Stolen kisses make my heart sing and she rubs my back to soothe the knifes that have landed in it on one too many occasions. She has rules that don't determine what I wear; they determine a dis-allowance of silent treatment or going to bed without kissing me goodnight. She fights with me over stolen bed covers, never stolen consent. On that beach, the wind blowing my hair, my knees trembling and my heart racing, my head spinning and her lips against mine. This is my new world. I call it the first world in which I have ever desired to stay alive.

SELFSONNET

By Ibn Qalam

The longest road to self is ever dark,
Obstructed by the walls of inner doubt,
And childish fears of dangers in the park,
Come night creeping when no one is about,
Awake the relentless agony screams,
Determined in its cruellest intent,
To scupper ones best intentions and dreams,
Consigning all hope to the same descent,
For courage is only a word until,
Its raised up and given determined mind,
The demons who decide you can't fulfil,
Ambition, volition the two combined.
Deep down inside where your secrets are held,
Is rebirth, hope and might unparalleled.

CRUSH MY TONGUE

By David Hollywood

Crush my tongue,
Pound my chest.
Press my heart,
Through sense oppressed.
Until the parts
that split from me,
Are squashed in thoughts
trounced nere to see.

Squeeze all I touch,
Constrict my taste.
Feel more to suffer,
Grasp to see,
That loves unbeen,
and deemed to dash
all thoughts that touch
our voices sights, which hear us be.

TO MATE JÁNOS, IN GRATITUDE

By Gabriella Garofalo

And now you come here, you, the end,
No, not the thriving seed
Where demise smiles by young minstrels-
Sorry? Days raging with life 'n' flowers?
You really think so? Honest?
Dream on, then, but don't forget
Those stoned souls,
The limbs left behind,
Drop those bloody shards, will you,
Stop throwing limbs to harvests of blood,
My love, my darling mine,
Stop straying from trees, from woods,
Can't you see your dancer dashing for a shelter?
So what? Bite your lips, my soul, and shut up,
Who's gonna draw the shadows now,
Maybe the creepers huddling up
In your womb, that kinky green trap?
Can't you see them tumbling, jerking,
Throwing you a blue funk anytime you slight contracted fires,
Anytime you give water to the distant shrubs,
Quick now, drop her if she stalks our souls,
If the moon's and women's eyes go slant
When giving blue water to weeds,
Or so fathers say when clawing shreds from the sky -
Is light whirling round? Thank God, the bloody-minded girl -
So dream on, scribbling lady,
Dream of branches' n', flowers,
But mind out, darling mine, life hates dreams' n' plans,
She gets mad at words whirling round
Like mad starving ravens -
You here, Caliban?
Oh, my friend so dear to the light,
Enjoy the show just for a change,
Let April show up in our caves
Of dark lust where you hear
God's bets'n' gambles all over the waves:
Who owns them, distress, or the zero hour, 3am?
Nope, girls staring wild, lusting for a sudden shot -
But I really dunno why some call it suicide
The blue wave that wipes away
The brittle white sand every now and then -

Our life, right?
Well, sorry, no, water you're doing,
And that extra flair to your smoothie -
Or so fathers say when hurling away heavenly shreds -
Is light whirling round?
Oh, look at those girls now, their shanks twinkling,
Shaking hair like Maenads, heads thrown back,
Look at the lady enjoying the show
While scribbling some words -
Is light whirling round?
Nope, she's chatting with someone
Who keeps mumbling words -
Entropy, a mate, dunno why.

SOMETIMES

By Beaton Galafa

Then, in some nights like these,
I feel cold and lonely in rooms engulfed
By frost and colds lost on their way to the mountain.
I dream of running to the station sometimes
With a train ticket and passport in hand
To board one back to the grave
Where all my brothers and sisters gather
Rich and poor, slave and master, preacher or sinner
Without hope or courage in light and darkness.

I want to fly over the hills and oceans again
Thinking, if the caves of the Himalayas and Andes
Swallow us from the glimpse of man's radar
Will the sins I committed when I was guilty
Before my blood tainted the wrecks and rocks
Count before the good Lord man extorted divinity from?

Only if I could swim or float on the blue ocean waters
I would wash away the dirt I see in my mind sometimes
Entering a parlour of racists, welcomed by monkeys and
Babies hanging on walls; marble glittering beneath
Poor black ladies paid to scream and exalt racist feudalists
Creeping into our forests in foggy nights,
Maiming and disfiguring mothers and babies
Even animals when man's blood alone can't wash
Nuba Mountains and the hot dry soils of Darfur clean.

First published on *Rejected Lit* in 2018.

THE JUNE PORCH - BEFORE THE CONCERT

By John Tunaley

I try and make my umbrella unfurl,
Who's stripped the porch? The rain keeps persisting,
The threatened concert is still proceeding
But when? The organiser's in a whirl.

I'm losing it too. I've some tiles broken,
A blocked downspout worsens my rising damp,
My treasured thinking leaks like this old gamp,
My spun-gold heart's turned to lump-lead token.

Denser than Heidegger, green-hooked bed-straw
Plasters the hedges. If pressed, I'd say
"Ontologically speaking I'm OK"
And stick to that despite the glaring flaw.

Weigh myself in? Scrap this mere subsistence?
Or hang on, and be grateful for existence?

First published in *The Light Programme,* a collection of 60 poems.

A SMARTPHONE ON A BROWN TABLE

By Eduard Schmidt-Zorner

The bistro was on the fourth floor of a building in Champigny-sur-Marne, in a quarter with colourful, mainly African markets, next to some rundown areas with advertisements for telephone sex via *Minitel* on phone boots, and a support of more than 60% for the Front National.

What first struck Aristide's eye when he arrived in the bistro, was a big painting in the vestibule. Underneath was a quote from Baudelaire:

> *O thou who knowest all, Hell's sovereign,*
> *Known healer of mankind's afflictions,*
> *Satan, have mercy on my long distress!*

The painting was of a desecrator, a green snake wound around his upper body, standing with raised hands in the yellow and red flames of hell. Lucifer with scarlet devil wings bent over the sinner pouring a cup of gall into his open mouth.

He distanced himself from this menacing and sombre message and sat down.

He had intended to continue reading the book of his favourite writer Michel Houellebecq, *The Elementary Particles* which describes the mercilessness of relations, the waste of the average life between illusory pleasure and fatal desire.

Aristide loved bistros and spent most of his free time in them. Drunks did not confront him, and he could read in peace. He loved the smell of pastry, chocolate, liqueurs. A bachelor, he enjoyed life, his independence and daily routine.

He took a seat, where he could watch the vestibule and the bistro entrance. He liked to watch people and analyse their habits, attitudes and reactions.

Near him sat a lady. She constantly checked her smart phone. She typed a message, dialled a number. Finally, she put the phone down with a sigh.

The owner of the bistro, a lady in her 60s, went over to her and their low voices gave the impression that they were friends. He could only get snippets of the conversation: "Alain left me... another woman... priest with magic powers .. he blessed me... I do not know what to do."

She stared again at the display in a dreamy mood, sunken into deep contemplation. The bistro owner returned to the counter but soon joined her again and the woman said: "I set him a deadline to make a decision. I gave him until 12 o'clock sharp."

It was five to twelve.

"Give him time," said the bistro owner, "pressure is no good." Aristide remembered the words of the philosopher Schopenhauer: *Il est temps de lâcher prise. It is time to let go.*

Aristide ordered another double espresso and a pastis. He looked again at the painting with the blurred flames of hell and the green, choking snake.

The chimes of the bells of Église de Saint-Joseph du Tremblay resounded, and the sound echoed from the walls of the high buildings.

The woman left and walked over to the vestibule windows.

The waiter delivered the coffee and pastis.

When Aristide looked up again, the woman was gone. Her smart phone and handbag left on the table.

Police and ambulance sirens sounded, and a man entered the bistro with wide-open arms, shouting: "A woman fell out of the window."

"Oh, Geneviève, no!"

The bistro owner and the customers ran to the vestibule window, looked down on the street and saw the twisted body of the woman, who had been sitting, alive, opposite Aristide, only a few minutes ago.

Into the stunned silence, the sound of the smart phone signalled an incoming message. While the customers were distracted, Aristide cast a quick glance at the display before the mobile went back into standby mode. It was an intrusion, but he was compelled to look.

The message read: "Sorry for being late, I am coming back to you. Forgive me. Alain."

The bistro owner looked over Aristide's shoulder. "You should not read other people's messages," she said.

"Look," Aristide said, holding the smart phone in front of her. When she read the message, she burst into tears.

"What misfortune. Never set a deadline; it is the line to death. Let fate take its course. Wait. Be patient. That was always my advice for Geneviève."

Aristide did not continue his reading, he could not concentrate, and as he left the building, the rain-washed blood and brain into the gully.

Would the husband of the woman realise that he had ruined her life before she ended it herself? Nothing was left but the message and a hope, which faded.

message has been sent

smart phone on a brown table
all in vain, too late.

AUTHOR'S NOTE: I had a long business contact with France and also a lot of private relations. I spent a lot of times in bistros and cafes, where I could watch people. Live is a stage play and if one is vigilant, a lot of things come to the surface and you hear a lot and share experience with others. There was a case in the quarter where I stayed in Paris and this tragedy was discussed with neighbours, I knew the protagonists but never knew her circumstances or problems. From this day on I was more careful with my judgement and I listened more to people, I took my time to listen and found out that listening and bringing people out of their isolation help and can prevent suicide.

TWO VOICES

By Lynda Tavakoli

If you listen really carefully you will hear it; the beating of my heart as its lifeblood gushes and slops against the ribs within my chest. Gradually it moves, thumping and pumping along the endless tubes and caverns of its journey to the centre of my mind. Thump, thump. Slop, slop. On it goes. Today and yesterday. Tomorrow and forever. Fear.

It is morning and although awake I allow my eyes to lie lazily shut and think of Jamie. He is my alter ego - the one who gets me out of bed in the morning, forcing me to dress, eat and wash my teeth. He is the voice inside keeping me sane, keeping me from the hopelessness that threatens to engulf me. Keeping me alive. Without him I would die.

I lie and listen to the soft movements from the kitchen below where my mother prepares breakfast for my father, trying not to waken me, her only son, in the room above. Ours is a small house and every creak, every click of a latch reverberates through its frame like ripples on a puddle. It means that when I cry I must be careful to pull the duvet tightly around my head. I am thirteen and crying I have learned, is only for wimps and nerds. Jamie never cries.

Muffled voices float upwards, seeping through the floorboards and I hear a door closing reluctantly downstairs. My father has gone to work. There was a time when he came to kiss me goodbye but once when he saw me scrunched within the duvet, he gently closed the door and never came again. This I understood and my love for him was never diminished because of it.

I hear my mother calling, "James, James, get up or you'll be late for school," and I bury myself still deeper beneath the covers, my head a throbbing mess of pain and tension. I hear Jamie's familiar voice telling me to shift myself. *"Come on James,"* he says, *"Get your act together – you've a bus to catch."* And because I know I have to, I comply.

It is October and autumn leaves crackle beneath the soles of my shiny black brogues. I am walking to catch the bus. Up Chester Avenue where I live, left at the end of the road and left again past the crumbling gateposts of the municipal park. I am in no hurry but Jamie is vying for attention in my head, encouraging me to speed up or I'll miss the bus. I see *them* before they see *me*. Fifty yards away standing in silhouette, lounging carelessly against the wooden bus shelter; smoke from their cigarettes drifting slowly outwards in staccatoed pockets of puff. I shuffle hesitantly forward until the one that is closest finally turns her eyes in my direction. And so it begins.

Jamie does not hesitate and I listen as he hisses the words I have heard in my head every day for nearly a year. *"You can do it today. Do it today."* But I am James and know that today will be the same as any other. Four pairs of eyes on me now and like heat seeking missiles they hone in on their target with perfect precision. Backs straighten and cigarette butts are obliterated beneath designer heels. The attack has begun.

"We like your shiny shoes James," she purrs, malice sticking like cream to her glossy lips. "Mummy clean them for you, did she?" and the others close in, smelling the scent of the kill and waiting excitedly for this morning's share of the spoils. I feel the moisture on my back as sweat sucks at the clean shirt which had, until a few minutes before, been crisp and dry. Instinctively my hand reaches in the pocket of my blazer to find the smooth comfort of the worry stone that awaits it there. My dummy substitute Jamie says.

Today I am saved by the bus as screeching brakes herald a sudden scramble for the doors. The survival of the fittest. Strong to the back seats; the weak, standing room only at the front. It takes twenty-two minutes to get from my stop to the school gates. I have timed it on my ultra-sophisticated, state of the art diver's watch my parents bought me for my birthday. It is hidden beneath the chewed cuffs of my grey school jumper and I imagine I can feel the pulse of it travelling up my arm, one second for two heartbeats to mark the growing apprehension churning in the pit of my stomach.

"Deep breaths," Jamie says, *"Deep breaths, we're nearly there."* But I cannot control my rising panic and feel the sour taste of sick rising up to fill the back of my throat. Up ahead I see the school gates and start holding my breath in an effort to prevent myself from throwing up. My lungs are burning but somehow I manage to hold on until the bus pulls up and we pour out onto the gum-peppered pavement now disgustingly covered with fresh spit. A large glob of it has hit me on the back of the neck, seeping down the collar of my shirt and resting at the top of my spine.

Jamie does not miss his chance *"Get the bastard's name James. Glob the bastard back."* But I can only feel the slow drag of my feet carrying me through the gates and into hell. The locker area buzzes. Forgotten rugby kits spill from holdalls in sweaty bundles and are kicked contemptuously across the parqueted floor. I listen as the smaller boys laugh at incomprehensible jokes while bigger boys delight in their telling, ensuring that every sexual nuance is exaggerated with the obligatory "f" word. A girl from my year walks by on her way to class and unexpectedly stops to ask, "Did you do that Maths homework James? Any chance of checking my answers with you?" Her name is Hazel. Her eyes are slightly crossed and she has the skinniest pair of legs I have ever seen, but she is nice. She has spoken to me before in the canteen. I say, "Later," and she continues to make headway down the corridor, her skirt swaying effortlessly as she walks.

"Oooh, James has got himself a little girlfriend then. Tasty bit of stuff, is she?" It is Billy Greg, king spitter and perpetrator of the Monday morning filthiest joke contest. I stand eyeball to eyeball with him, his lips practically touching my own he is so close.

"*Tell him to piss off James,*" urges Jamie from somewhere faraway in my head. I want to. In fact I want to hit Billy Greg so hard that I smash his beautiful straight teeth right to the back of his throat. But I can't, and I won't, and I know I never will.

"She's not my girlfriend," I tell him, reaching quickly to close the locker door and make my escape. It is a mistake. Like a magpie attracted to some shiny object, Billy glimpses the watch and grabs my wrist like a vice. His fingers are unbelievably soft and I sense Jamie sniggering at this unexpected femininity.

"And what have we got here then James?" Billy snarls, "A nice new watch from mummy and daddy. You kept that one a bit quiet." I am getting scared now, the smell of the locker room is overpowering, the tension unbearable. Some of the boys have gone off to classes but none of those who have stayed will champion me. I am on my own with a stupid voice in my head and a useless body to go with it. The vice–like grip tightens.

"Give me the watch nerd," Billy whispers, his breath hot in my ear, the words hardly discernible. "Nice and graciously so nobody gets the idea that maybe you didn't want to. Give it like a present." I do not want to relinquish the watch. It is the only possession I have managed to keep secret and I do not know how to explain its disappearance to my parents. Jamie screams at me in the distance, "*James. James. Punch his lights out. Keep the watch. It's ours. It's ours,*" and for a fleeting, wonderful moment I almost feel like I could do it. The bell rings, the moment is gone and my bravery banished by the reality of an ever-present threat even Jamie cannot erase. Slowly I remove the precious present from my wrist and place it into the hand of my tormentor.

"*Coward,*" accuses Jamie. He will not speak to me until later when his disgust at my weakness has been diminished. Billy saunters nonchalantly away and the others, disappointed that there has been no bloodletting this morning, hurriedly make their way to class. My eyes remain dry. There are no tears left for me to cry. I am thirteen years old and I do not understand how it has come to this. I wonder what it was, the terrible thing that I must have done in some past life to pay such penance now. My mum and dad tried to help when they began noticing little tell-tale signs indicating that all was not well with my life at school. Phone calls were made, meetings arranged and strategies put in place, but none of it did any good. It only made things worse and in the end I pretended the bullying had stopped. The only one I really share it with now is Jamie and even he becomes angry and frustrated at my inability to retaliate. Like today when he has remained silent since I gave up the watch and my isolation grows more intolerable as the day wears on. I speak to no one and even Hazel has forgotten her earlier request to cross check our homework. It was such a little thing but I feel the hurt of her forgetfulness acutely and the fear in me melts into a kind of resigned despair.

Today the journey home allows some respite. The big, tough, macho boys remain in school with the big, tough, macho rugby playing teachers. The girls don their makeup and gossip together in groups on street corners. Nobody is interested in James Baker anymore. Our house is empty. My mother has left the key for me beneath a flowerpot and I let myself in at four fourteen by the hall clock. In an hour mum will return from the charity shop where she helps out but in the meantime I can be relied upon to make a snack for myself and start some homework. The house smells nice. Everything is tidy. Outside I hear the familiar noise of the traffic trundling down our road.

Jamie begins to forgive me and starts up a conversation in my head, *"Tell them you lost it at PE James. You can try and get it back tomorrow,"* but his voice is coming from a distant place and I am not listening. I go to the closet beneath the stairs. My dad's big box of tools is there and I rummage to find the old rope he saves 'just in case'. I wonder if it is long enough.

Thump, thump. Slop, slop. Strange that the fear is still here when I feel nothing but absolute calm. Strange, too, that for the first time Jamie has begun to panic. *"Don't James. It only means that they've won,"* but I know this is not true. I tie an end of the rope to the top of the banister and tug it tightly, feeling my weight on it and testing its strength. I make a kind of noose with the other end and place it over my head. Will it hurt? Will it be immediate? It doesn't matter. "It's okay Jamie," I say. "It's really okay". And I step out fearlessly into wonderful oblivion.

First published in Lynda's short story anthology *A Cold White Moon*.

Interview with Lynda

Tell me a little about yourself Lynda

I was a Special Needs teacher for four decades on and off, employed in both the Primary and Secondary sectors across the UK, so have been involved with children from a very young age right through to the teenage years. My job was primarily focused on the literacy and numeracy skills of the children but increasingly it also included pastoral care and dealing with the sometimes difficult social circumstances many of my pupils had to cope with. As such, a number of these experiences provided me with better insight into some of the problems many of our young people now have to confront.

As a parallel job I was a Non-Executive director of one of the Health Trusts here in Northern Ireland, and this complemented my teaching role greatly as it involved working in partnership with Social Services on many occasions. It gave me an invaluable opportunity to link the two vocations as they obviously overlap each other extensively. It would be true to say that quite often I found there was not nearly enough communication between schools and social services but with lack of funding inevitably being a huge issue, it's desperately hard to get things right and to please everyone. Consequently, this can have a detrimental effect on children of all ages.

And how does this career experience relate to your writing?

I came to writing quite by accident really. Sadly, one of my friends had died of breast cancer while I was abroad, and I wrote a very personal and honest piece about our relationship (I also had breast cancer) which I sent to a local newspaper back home. To my surprise, they not only published it, but asked me to do a series of articles concerning human interest stories, and that's where my writing career began. I will always be indebted to *The Belfast Telegraph* for their faith in me at that time and for accepting other pieces throughout the years. It is important for me to be honest in my journalistic writings as I value my integrity above all else but I do worry these days about offering an opinion in the public domain (and ultimately social media) when there are so many people out there seemingly waiting to take offence.

I would later gravitate to the more creative writing side of things and begin to write fiction. Here, there was much more scope to use my imagination and dramatic licence comes into play constantly, so although the situations I put my characters in are often based on reality, they are not based on any real people. Something I have discovered about myself is that I like to take on uncomfortable subjects or themes that can be difficult to confront and these would include suicide, euthanasia or the loss of a child, for example.

And how does this relate to your piece?

The short story *Two Voices* was certainly not written about any specific situation I had experienced personally. It was more that I was trying to understand the thinking of any child who might have found themselves in an unbearable situation for which there was no obvious solution. As someone who has received counselling myself in the past, I knew that feelings of helplessness or hopelessness can be destructive in the most powerful way and sometimes lead to tragic consequences. Nowadays there is much more open discussion around mental health and therefore better awareness of the help available. This story, when I wrote it (before the real advent of social media), was an attempt to tackle the scenario of a child unable or unwilling to ask for help and although it was difficult to write I didn't want to shy away from the truth that suicides can happen when all hope appears lost to an individual. For James, the protagonist in my story, life had become unbearable because of bullying at school, and although I have never in all my teaching career been witness to anything close to this scenario, the reality of it is that there is bullying in every school to some extent. Teachers generally do what they can but sometimes it's just not possible to spot a pupil who is going through inner turmoil as they are often extremely adept at hiding their emotions. James is loved. He comes from a caring family. He is respectful and maybe a little old-fashioned but he doesn't fit in and for this reason alone he is targeted. The sad thing is that for the perpetrators of the bullying, taunting James is only a transitory 'bit of fun' and afterwards they carry on with their everyday business, but for James it is an all-consuming ordeal that he believes he can never escape from. The conflicting voices in his head are his means of trying to cope when really he should be offering those thoughts up to another person – someone who will simply listen without judgement and not even necessarily offer advice. The fact that James blames himself (albeit illogically) for his situation and has internalised his emotional problems, means that he has isolated himself from the people who could help and actually give him the guidance and empathy he needs to find a way forward. The story could have ended more positively than it did of course, and perhaps if I rewrote it now I might give it a more enigmatic conclusion. However, at the time of writing, it felt like an honest attempt to face the reality that in this life not everything has a happy ending.

Do you think just having the time to listen to other people is important?

Yes, of course. I am not a counsellor, a psychotherapist or a doctor trained in the area of mental health. But I don't think you necessarily need to be any of these things to be a good listener which is perhaps the most important healing skill of all. During my teaching career I have come across children who just needed someone to hear them, and to be told that it's okay to voice their fears or misgivings. Regardless of race, creed, sexual orientation, social background etc. we all face differing degrees of problems and challenges as we go through our lives and depression can occur for all sorts of reasons sometimes completely out of the blue. It can be triggered by any number of things but I imagine that loneliness is high up there in the list of causes and I don't just mean the loneliness of being on your own. Even in an environment of supportive family and friends one can experience what I would call 'loneliness of the soul' and that's a hard frame of mind to claw your way out of on your own.

Do you think social media plays a part in this?

Nowadays it's hard to ignore the growing issues surrounding social media. It can be a means of great good if used responsibly of course, but increasingly it seems to have taken over our lives in a way that could never have been foreseen even a few years ago, (in *Two Voices* I didn't tackle this issue specifically as the story was set in a time prior to the present dilemmas that exist). I do feel really sorry for the younger generation these days though in that there is constant pressure to comply with what some total stranger has deemed the 'norm' (when it is actually nowhere near the 'norm'). Also the constant and incessant need to be on the other end of a phone checking for messages, *'likes'* and so on is gradually making us lose the ability to connect properly face to face. Nothing can replace a human touch that says; "You're doing okay. You're not alone. You don't need to be something that you're not." Sadly, I don't see a solution to this any time soon unless people start to communicate with each other away from a flat screen.

Do you have any advice you can give others feeling suicidal or self-harming?

I'm very reluctant to offer advice to anyone who might be suffering from depression or mental health issues, because every case is so individual and personal. But I do think that no matter how bad something may seem at that moment in time when you feel all is lost, it *can* get better if you can only give it more time. I don't mean to be flippant when I say that any situation can look very different in the morning, for actually I've found this to be true. Even a few minutes of 'parking' something can change the way you feel about it and taking one tiny step at a time allows you the space to seek for the help and support you need. We could do worse than remember the words of the wonderful singer-song writer, poet and novelist Leonard Cohen:

"There is a crack in everything. That's how the light gets in."

And I truly believe that there is light in all our lives if only we can give it the opportunity to shine.

CONTRIBUTORS...

ABIGAIL GEORGE
Pushcart Prize-nominated for her fiction *Wash Away My Sins,* Abigail George is a South African-based blogger at Goodreads (link on Piker Press), essayist, poet, playwright, grant, novella and short story writer. She briefly studied film at the Newtown Film and Television School in Johannesburg. She is the recipient of two writing grants from the National Arts Council in Johannesburg, one from the Centre for the Book in Cape Town and another from ECPACC (Eastern Cape Provincial Arts and Culture Council) in East London. Her writing has appeared numerous times in print in South Africa, in various anthologies in Africa, the UK and the States, and online in e-zines based across Africa, Asia, Australia, Canada, Europe, Ireland, and the United States. She is the writer of eight books including essays, life writing, memoir pieces, novellas, poetry and a self-published story collection. She lives, works, and is inspired by the people and mountains of the Eastern Cape of Southern Africa. She is the poetry editor at *AfricanWriter.com* and an editor at Mwanaka Media and Publishing. She was born in 1979 and is of mixed race descent. This has informed a large part of her writing. Storytelling for her has always been a phenomenal way of communicating. She has lived for most of her life in the Northern Areas of Port Elizabeth. Her latest book is *The Scholarship Girl* (Mwanaka Media and Publishing, 2019, edited by Tendai Rinos Mwanaka). She has two chapbooks forthcoming in 2019/2020; *Of Bloom and Smoke* (Mwanaka Media and Publishing, 2019, edited by Antonio Garcia) and *The Anatomy of Melancholy* (Praxis Magazine, 2019/2020, edited by JK Anowe).
E: abigailgeorge79@gmail.com
FB: @abigailgeorgewriter
Blog: www.goodreads.com/author/show/5174716.Abigail_George

BARBARA HAWTHORN
Barbara lives in Auckland, New Zealand. She is a retired teacher (Mathematics) with a lifelong addiction to writing. Currently a member of International Writers' Workshop, Northcote, New Zealand, Barbara is a musician, playing mandola in The Auckland Mandolinata Orchestra.
E: john.hawthorn@xtra.co.nz

BEATON GALAFA
Beaton Galafa is a Malawian writer. His works have appeared in *Stuck in the Library, Transcending the Flame, 300K Anthology, Home/Casa, Betrayal, The Seasons, Empowerment, The Elements, BNAP 2017*

Anthology, BNAP 2018 Anthology, Writing Grandmothers, Writing Politics and Knowledge Production, Better Than Starbucks, Love Like Salt Anthology, Literary Shanghai, Mistake House, Fourth & Sycamore, The Blue Tiger Review, The Wagon Magazine, Rejected Lit, Every Writer's Resource, Eunoia Review, The Bombay Review, Nthanda Review, Kalahari Review, The Maynard, Birds Piled Loosely, Atlas and Alice, South 85 Journal and elsewhere.
E: beatongalafa@gmail.com

BEE PARKINSON-CAMERON

Bee is a writer of poetry, short stories and plays. She focuses on exploring love in all its forms, the oppositions of life and death and the nature of humanity and what it means to be human. She is passionate about issues such as mental health, domestic abuse, euthanasia, abortion and human sexuality. Bee's work has been published in several anthologies including Collections Of Poetry And Prose's Love, War, Travel and Happy, The Challenges Of Finding Love, and Uncovered Voices. She has also produced two plays; The Divine Comedy Show in March 2017 and The Journey Home a play about domestic abuse in November 2018.
E: beeparkinsoncameron@gmail.com
FB : @bee.parkinsoncameron

BERNADETTE PEREZ

"What I create today is who I am at this moment. If my art can touch one soul, save one life, touch one heart then my craft has conveyed it's message." In 1990, Bernadette received the Silver Poet Award from World of Poetry. Her work has appeared in The Wishing Well; Musings in 2010, Small Canyons Anthology in 2013 and in Poems 4 Peace in 2014. Contribution to La Familia: La Casa de Colores, and Fix and Free Anthologies. Winner of the Wagner Society of Santa Fe Audience Favourite 'Write Your Own Prize Song' and included in the mega-unity poem by Juan Felipe. Bernadette was also included in The Americans Museum Inscription by Shinpei Takeda, and has been published in over 100 publications between 2015-2018 including a number of Collections of Poetry and Prose. When she is not writing, Bernadette works full time as a Corporate Success Leader and balancing her love of poetry as the New Mexico State Poetry Society President.
E: bpburritos@aol.com

BILL COX

Bill lives in Aberdeen, Scotland. He started writing in 2014 and won the 2016/17 One Giant Read flash fiction competition. He has had work published in a number of anthologies and online. He describes his writing as *'inspiring and transcendent'*, but then he would say that, wouldn't he?

E: malphesius@yahoo.com

Blog: www.northeastnotesblog.wordpress.com

CHRYS SALT

Chrys is a seasoned performer and a widely published and anthologized poet. She has performed in Festivals across the UK in Europe, America, Canada, Finland and India, and written in almost every genre except the novel. Numerous awards include a National Media Award, an Arts and Business Award, Several Writing Bursaries and a Fringe First from The Edinburgh Festival. She has published seven books for actors (Pub: Methuen Drama) and nine poetry collections (publishers various). Her poem *The Burning* was selected as one of the Best Scottish Poems 2012. Her pamphlet *Weaver of Grass* was shortlisted for the Callum MacDonald Memorial Award. Her most recent collection, *The Punkawallah's Rope* is rooted in a trip to India in 2015 to appear at The Kolkata Literary Festival. She received a Creative Scotland Bursary in 2017 to research material in The Yukon for her forthcoming collection about the Klondike Gold Rush. She will be The International Poet at the Tasmanian Poetry Festival 2019. Chrys was awarded an MBE in the Queen's Birthday Honours List 2014 for Services to The Arts. She is Artistic Director of BIG LIT: The Stewartry Book Festival, a five day literary festival in SW Scotland now in its ninth year.

E: chrys@chryssalt.com

W: www.chryssalt.com

W: www.biglit.org

CYNTHIA MORRISON

Cynthia resides within the Bermuda Triangle. She is a writer and an award-winning playwright with theatrical works featured Off-Broadway in New York City. She is also a graduate of the Burt Reynolds Institute and Palm Beach State College. Her stage play *Words with a Mummy* is published inside *21st Century Literature from the Philippines and the World* as a textbook lesson in *"adaptation of a play from literature."* She is also a Faulkner Society Finalist.

E: nogunshier@aol.com

W: www.cynthiamorrison.yolasite.com

DAVID A BANKS

David escaped from the confines of academic writing and now roams the fresh pastures of poetry and theatre, where he encounters far less bull. He regularly earwigs on conversations in a number of cafe haunts under the guise of 'research'. When not reading or writing, he

has been known to make wooden dolls' houses, manufacture interesting pieces of firewood on a lathe, or spend many hours in the garden planning what he might do next time the weather conditions are absolutely perfect. He lives by the wise words of a respected friend who advised that most work activities should be given '*a good coat of looking-at*' before commencing.
E: traveldab@gmail.com

DAVID LOHREY

David's plays have been produced in Switzerland, Croatia, and Lithuania. In the US, his poems can be found at the *RavensPerch, New Orleans Review, Nice Cage*, and *Panoplyzine*. Internationally, his work appears in☐journals located in India, Ireland, Malawi, Hungary, and Singapore. His fiction can be seen at *Dodging the Rain, Terror House Magazine*, and *Literally Stories*. David's collection of poetry, *MACHIAVELLI'S BACKYARD*, was published by Sudden Denouement Publishers. He lives in Tokyo.
E: lohr_burgh@hotmail.com

DAVID HOLLYWOOD

David lives in Switzerland and is married with four children. His particular interest is in developing a public enthusiasm for poetry among those who aspire too appreciate the genre, but haven't yet made the leap into writing or proclaiming their verse. As a result, he founded, and for four years directed The Colours of Life poetry festival's in Bahrain, and subsequently worked upon the same in Antigua, The West Indies and Ireland before moving to Switzerland. He is the author of an eclectic collection of poems titled *Waiting Spaces* plus contributed to *My Beautiful Bahrain, Poetic Bahrain, More of My Beautiful Bahrain* and was the in-house poet for *Bahrain Confidential* magazine and, as a result, he is one of the most widely read Western poets in The Middle East. He is also a regular literary critic for *Taj Mahal Review*, plus an essayist on the subject of poetry appreciation. He has been accredited with membership of The Society of Classical Poets. There are plans for a new collection of poetry and essays to be released shortly.
E: davidhollywood23@hotmail.com

DONNA ZEPHRINE

Donna was born in Harlem New York and grew up in Bay Shore, Long island. She went to Brentwood High School, graduated from Columbia University School of Social Work in May 2017, and currently works for the New York State Office of Mental Health at Pilgrim Psychiatric Center Outpatient SOCR (State Operated Community Residence). She is a combat veteran who completed two tours in Iraq. She was on

active duty army stationed at Hunter Army Airfield 3rd Infantry Division as a mechanic. Since returning home, Donna enjoys sharing her experiences and storytelling through writing. Donna's stories most recently have been published in *Qutub Minar Review, Bards Initiative, Radvocate, Oberon*, Long Island Poetry Association and *The Mighty*. Donna has participated in various veteran writing workshops throughout NYC. Recently Donna was featured USA Warrior stories took part in Warrior Chorus and Decruit which encourage self-expression through looking as classical literature and performing it while relating it to your own life with war and trauma. Currently Donna is studying for her licensing in social work. Donna is always seeking new experiences to learn such as Toast Masters which focuses on public speaking. She is involved in World Team Sports, Wounded Warrior Project and Team Red White and Blue. In her spare time Donna plays sled hockey for the Long Island Rough Riders.
E: kauldonna@yahoo.com

EBUWA OHENHEN
"I am from Nigeria. I write poetry, I edit works of literature by other writers and I proofread works of literature too. I have made it my life's mission to fight depression, injustice and cultism in any way I can - usually with my poems. I hate injustice, pride, dishonesty, hypocrisy and oppression."
E: ebuwaaiseosaohenhen@gmail.com
FB: @upcominggenius
Instagram: @iam_d_anomaly

EDUARD SCHMIDT-ZORNER
Eduard is an artist and a translator and writer of poetry, crime novels and short stories. He is writing haibun, tanka, haiku and poetry in four languages: English, French, Spanish and German, and holds workshops on Japanese and Chinese style poetry and prose. He is a member of four writer groups in Ireland, and lives in County Kerry, Ireland since more than 25 years, and is a proud Irish citizen, born in Germany. He was published in 43 anthologies, literary journals and broadsheets in UK, Ireland, Canada and USA. Eduard also writes under his pen name Eadbhard McGowan.
E: EadbhardMcGowan@gmx.com
W: www.eadbhardmcgowan.wixsite.com/website

GABRIELLA GAROFALO
Born in Italy some decades ago, Gabriella fell in love with the English language at six when she started writing poems (in Italian), and is the author of *Lo sguardo di Orfeo, L'inverno di vetro, Di altre stelle polari* and *Blue branches.*

GUY MORRIS

"I'm an ageing truck driver, living in the north west of England, and have done a multitude of jobs since leaving school including Casino Croupier, police officer, security guard and was once a Strippergram! I've written poetry from an early age."

E: sirromyug@hotmail.com

HANNAH LOUISE MACFARLANE

Hannah was born and raised in a small sea side town in Scotland and is a writer, director, actress, script writer, teacher, and pretty much every other creative entity she can aim to be. Discovering the art of writing in her younger years influenced the creative professional route she is venturing on, with a passion and commitment to implementing real change in the world through education and a multitude of art forms.

E: hannahlouise-macfarlane@hotmail.com

Instagram: @hannahlouisemacfarlane

HEERA NAWAZ

Heera had been working as a teacher at Cambridge School, K. R. Puram, Bengaluru. She is also a writer, and has been writing feature articles, stories, poems (both rhyming and non-rhyming), plays and songs for the past 30 years. She wrote her first poem when she was an 8-year-old student in New York. There has been no looking back, and she writes prolifically besides reading voraciously. She recently won an Award for being *The Times* of India Best NIE Teacher Co-ordinator (which involves writing and editing creative work and poetry) from over 250 schools in Bengaluru. One of her prose pieces has been accepted by the Indian edition of the *Reader's Digest*, and she has been interviewed twice by *NDTV Good Times*.

E: nawazheera@gmail.com

IBN QALAM

I live in Bahrain, in the Gulf, am married for 25 years and have three children.

E: nader@ksdibahrain.com

JO WILSON-RIDLEY

Jo's day job is to convince motorists to drive safely. Never short of work, in the evening hours Jo writes and performs poetry. Jo has been published in *five bells, fourW* new writing anthologies, *Feast of Poetry, Not Very Quiet Journal* and on a postcard with the Ekphrasis Poetry Competition. Performing poetry - Jo has been a State Finalist in the Australian Poetry Slam in 2011, 2012, 2013 & 2015. Jo lives with her family in Queanbeyan, NSW, and practices poetry lines while

walking the family cattle dog along the Queanbeyan River. Jo still picks up the best performance lines from sitting on the sidelines listening to the cheering as her teenage sons play basketball & AFL for Queanbeyan Tigers.
E: jo_wilson_ridley@hotmail.com

JOHN TUNALEY
Born in Manchester in 1945 (father; foundry hand, mother;crane-driver), John now lives in Robin Hoods' Bay, North Yorkshire. He's in a few writing groups plus a painting group... a tai-chi group... a music group... his French class... then there's Open Gardens to help sort out for June (proceeds to the Alzheimer's Society) and the grandchildren who demand he plays with them.... he gets no rest. He enjoys the 'anthology' approach, and tends to stick to sonnets as the form exercises some control over his worse excesses.
E: johntunaley@yahoo.co.uk

JOHN-KARL STOKES
John-Karl is internationally known as one of Australia's most daring and interesting of poets and librettists. He's on a campaign to bring back plain-speaking to the most emotional writings in English.
E: johnstokespoet@me.com
W: www.JohnKarlStokes.com

KATRINA CATTERMOLE
Katrina lives with her Siberian husky Kodee in Noffolk, England. This is her first piece of writing based on an abusive and controlling relationship.
E: katrina007@hotmail.co.uk

KIMMY ALAN
Kimmy is a wannabe poet from the land of Lake Woebegone. A retired steel worker who was diagnosed with Stage 4 cancer, Kimmy pursed his love of poetry as a distraction while undergoing chemo and radiation. For him, poetry has proven to be a powerful catharsis as he is currently in remission. When he isn't writing he spends time with his four wonderful nieces, whom he says *"are driving him to pieces."*
E: kimmyalan@outlook.com

LINDA M. CRATE
Linda is a Pennsylvanian native born in Pittsburgh yet raised in the rural town of Conneautville. She is a two-time push cart nominee. Her poetry, short stories, articles, and reviews have been published in a myriad of magazines both online and in print. She has six

published chapbooks *A Mermaid Crashing Into Dawn* (Fowlpox Press - June 2013), *Less Than A Man* (The Camel Saloon - January 2014), *If Tomorrow Never Comes* (Scars Publications, August 2016), *My Wings Were Made to Fly* (Flutter Press, September 2017), *Splintered with Terror* (Scars Publications, January 2018), *More Than Bone Music* (Clare Songbirds Publishing House, March 2019), and one micro-chapbook *Heaven Instead* (Origami Poems Project, May 2018). She is also the author of the novel *Phoenix Tears* (Czykmate Books, June 2018).
E: veritaserumvial@hotmail.com
FB: @Linda-M-Crate-129813357119547
Instagram: @authorlindamcrate
Twitter: @thysilverdoe

LINDA-ANN LOSCHIAVO
LindaAnnis a dramatist, author, theatre critic, and poet. *Conflicted Excitement* [Red Wolf Editions, 2018] is her latest poetry chapbook. Her poetry has been published in M*easure, Italian American, Owen Wister Review, PIF, The Cape Rock, Lullwater Review, Mused, Ink & Letters, Peacock Journal, Not Very Quiet, Sweet Deluge, Rue Scribe, Windhover,* etc. and has won competitions in the USA and Canada. Her play *Naked Came the Painting* will be staged in Westchester County, NY in a 500-seat theatre in May 2019. Her collaborative non-fiction work on prejudice (published in the USA by Macmillan) will be released in an Italian version in Rome, Italy by Arachne Editrice in May 2019.
E: nonstopny@aol.com
Blog: www.MaeWest.blogspot.com
Twitter: @Mae_Westside

LYNDA TAVAKOLI
Lynda, author of two novels and the short story collection, *Under a Cold White Moon*, facilitates a creative writing class in Lisburn, Northern Ireland. Her poetry and prose have been broadcast on both BBC Radio Ulster and RTE Sunday Miscellany. Literary successes include poetry and short story prizes at Listowel, the Mencap short story competition, and the *Mail on Sunday* novel competition. Having recently returned from Oman, she is presently working towards a debut poetry collection. Lynda has facilitated prose recitals commemorating the anniversary of the sinking of The Titanic and edited the prose and poetry anthology *Linen* for the Irish Linen Museum.
E: lyndatavakoli@aol.com

MALCOLM JUDD

I have been writing poetry for around 20 years. Most of my work, although not all, has been written whilst suffering depression and mental illness.

E: maccyj22@hotmail.com

MALIHA HASSAN

Maliha is poet from Pakistan. Her poems give a food for thought and motivates the thinking process. She has done Masters in English Literature and Language and Masters in TEFL. Being associated with the teaching profession for the last three decades she got an opportunity to observe people and their surroundings,hence reflected in her poems.

E: mlh.hassan@gmail.com

MARGARETH STEWART

Margareth is the pen name of Mônica Mastrantonio PhD, author at Amazon, Kobo and Smashwords. Mônica's a mum of three, loves jogging, reading, writing, sunbathing, travelling, meeting people. Always happy, always forward, 101% Italian.

E: joysince1969@outlook.com
FB: @AuthorMargarethStewart
Instagram: @author_margarethstewart

MARK BLICKLEY

Mark is a proud member of the Dramatists Guild and PEN American Centre. He is the author of *Sacred Misfits* (Red Hen Press), *Weathered Reports: Trump Surrogate Quotes from the Underground* (Moira Books) and the just published text based art book, *Dream Streams* (Clare Songbirds Publishing). His video, *Widow's Peek: The Kiss of Death*, was selected to the 2018 International Experimental Film Festival in Bilbao, Spain. He is a 2018 Audie Award Finalist for his contribution to the original audio book, *Nevertheless We Persisted*.

E: lickwords@yahoo.com

MARY ANNE ZAMMIT

Mary Anne is a graduate from the University of Malta in Social Work, in Probation Services, in Diplomatic Studies and in Masters in Probation. She has also obtained a Diploma in Freelance and Feature Writing from the London School of Journalism, and paints, writes poetry, novels and articles both in Maltese and in English. She is the author of three fiction books in Maltese. The first book was *Id-Dell ta' l-Eżmeraldi*, and *Ir-Raġel l-Iswed*, the latter was awarded a prize by MAPA (Maltese Association of Authors and Publishers) This was

followed by a fiction book with the title *Stupru* (*Rape*). In 2005 Marie Anne attended for a script writing workshop in Sitges, Spain. The book was presented in the literary section in the festival; Woman Creators of the Two Seas. Woman and Tradition, held in Thessaloniki, Greece between the 28 August and 04 September 2006. The Festival was organized by the Unesco Centre for Women and Peace in the Balkans. In 2008 the novel *Torn Velvet* was published and exhibited at the New Title Show Case at the London Book Fair between the 14 and 16 April 2008. The same book was published by the Mental Health Group with the title *Shattered Wings*. In 2009 Mary Anne's fourth book in Maltese *Tfal Misruqa, (Kidnapped Children)* a novel about the reality of missing children and child pornography, was published. In 2009 the Marie Anne's short story *My Son, My Past* was highly commended in the Aesthetica Annual Creative Competition UK. In 2010 two poems were published in the *Strand book for International Poetry* by Strand Publishers UK. In 2015, the novel *Dawn in Seville* was published. In 2015 one of Mary Anne's poem has been set to music and performed during the Mdina Cathedral Art Biennale by Maestro Reuben Pace. Mary Anne's literary work was also featured in *Literature Today, Volume 4, 5, and 6*. Other two poems were published in 2016 in *Taj Mahal Review* Volume 15, published by Cyberwit India. One other poem was published in the *New English Verse* in 2016, and in *Praxis on Line Magazine for Arts and Literature,* and in *Collections of Poetry and Prose*. Other poetry was published in 2017 in *International Contemporary Poetry Volume* 4. In 2018 other poetry was included in the *Qutub Minor Review Vol. 1.* In 2019 another poem was published in *Literature Today Volume 8.* Mary Anne is also artist and had participated in various art exhibitions both locally and abroad. In 2018 Mary Anne has been awared I-Artista dell Anno at the Mezzujosu International Art Exhibition in Mezzujosu, Sicily and awarded again in an another International Art Exhibition in Comiso, in September. Mary Anne's art has also been featured in Autumn edition 2018 of *Art Ascent* and in *Rejoinder Journal* online published by the Institute for Research on Women, and in *The Universal Sea, The Art and Innovation Movement against water Pollution.*
E: mariefrances3@gmail.com

MAY MATHEW MANOJ

"I am May Manoj, born in Kerala on the 9th of October, 1983. Travelling to Bahrain at the age of 4, I resided there for 30 years, completing my schooling and post graduation there. I worked for more than 10 years as a French and English teacher in Bahrain, subsequently writing poetry. I am married to a church minister, Manoj Abraham, and have three lovely boys Elijah, Jonathan and

Faith. I have contributed to several poetry collections and authored a book; *Rose Garden of Love.*
E: princesse.amie@gmail.com

MICHAEL J. ROLLINS

"I was born, and have lived most of my life, in Barrow in Furness, Cumbria, in the North West of England, working in the local shipyard until leaving to train as an English teacher. I now work in the British School of Al Khobar, in Saudi Arabia. Although I have written poetry for many years, I have only recently begun to work on short stories. The writers whose stories have encouraged me to want to write include Peter Straub, Haruki Marukami, Cormac McCarthy and Leonard Cohen."
E: mikeyrollins@yahoo.com

MTENDE WEZI NTHARA

Mtende lives and writes from Malawi. She currently works with the Catholic University of Malawi as an Associate Lecturer in the English and Communication Studies Department. An avid reader of all things literary, some of her poetry features at *Kalahari Review* and *Nthanda Review.*
E: mtendewezi@gmail.com

NIKORI ESE PRAISE

Nikori is a final year female student of the department of Mass Communication, University of Benin.
E: esenikori@gmail.com
Instagram: @ehssay
Twitter: @ehssayy

NILANJANA BOSE

Nilanjana is a parent, writer, poet, blogger and a market research professional. Born in Kolkata, India, brought up in New Delhi and West Africa, her mailing address has changed some fifteen times so far, and she is always ready for the next change. She believes in travelling light, and a sense of humour, along with the passport, is top on her packing list. Dipping into other cultures and countries, whether as an expat resident or a tourist, refreshes her writing muscles. She speaks English, Bengali and Hindi; and understands more Arabic than she can account for. She has a first class degree in Maths from Delhi University, a diploma in Marketing from Chartered Institute of Marketing, UK; and has lived/worked in India, Nigeria, Bahrain, UAE and Egypt. She celebrates the diverse range of cultural environments that she has experienced and her ability to navigate different landscapes of language, beliefs and customs. She has

written over two thousand poems and hundreds of short stories, flash fiction and essays; her writing is informed by her travels as well as her own heritage. Her poems, short stories, essays and travel memoirs have been published in both print and on-line. Her first book was a collection of short fiction in Bengali called *Seemaheen Bidesh (Foreign without Borders)*. Her work has appeared in print in *Ananda Lipi* (US), *Sabaya* (Bahrain), in multi-author anthologies like *Social Potpourri – An Anthology* and *10 Love Stories* released by Indiblogger and Harper Collins India in 2015, as well as online in e-zines like *eFiction India*. She was a contributing editor in *Inner Child* magazine (US) with her own byline Passport to Our World - a travel feature which ran to a twenty-four part series.
E: nilabose306b@gmail.com
Blog: Madly-in-Verse

NOOR YOUSIF
Noor is a Mass Communication student in University of Bahrain and a freelancer journalist. She has written several articles for non-profit national organizations whose aims are to approach audiences in order to raise awareness about culture, physical and intellectual disabilities. Additionally, she volunteers with international organizations working in different programs encouraging society's acceptance of different nationalities. Furthermore, she coordinates and organizes international youth forums aiming to create an environment where both youth and leaders from diverse backgrounds can cross-pollinate ideas, share insights, and gain new perspectives in order to create actionable outcomes to push the world forward.
E: noormyousif@gmail.com
Instagram: @itsnoor_97
Twitter @icedchaihaleeb

NURAH HARUN
I am a Bangladeshi Indian writer/poet, brought up in the Middle East and currently residing in Bahrain. Nur means light in Arabic. And I shed light on social issues by lending words to stories and poetry about being human. In our confusing world, writing and other creative outlets helps me deal with our collective madness.
E: fatema.zohra89@gmail.com
Instagram: @bangaligypsy

PAMELA SCOTT
Pamela lives in Glasgow, UK. Her work has appeared in various magazines including *Buckshot* Magazine, *Brilliant Flash Fiction*, *A Quiet Courage*, *Allegro Poetry Magazine* and *Dream Catcher*. She has also featured in *Collections of Poetry and Prose* and Indigo Dreams

Press. She is working on her third novel.
E: pamelascottwriter@yahoo.com
FB: @pcottwriter
Twitter: @pscottwriter
Blog: www.365writingdays.wordpress.com
Pinterest: @pamelascottwriter

PARVINDER KAUR
A 19 year-old student of English language and literature in Bahrain, and an artist with a passion for poetry and illustration, Parvinder commits to temper with set boundaries, and is inspired by every element in nature.
E: kaurp133345@gmail.com
Blog: www.theinkedwolf.wordpress.com
Twitter: @_KaurParvinder

PASITHEA CHAN
Pasithea is a budding Lebanese-Filipina poet who enjoys writing her impressions in symbolism, laced with philosophy and psychology. She writes in various styles but prefers pieces that have double meanings to allow a reader to delve deeper into her works.
E: Shirochan1984@gmail.com

RICHARD GOSS
Richard suffers with Post Traumatic Stress Disorder (PTSD) and complex depression due to time spent in the British army, where he served for 10 years including tours in Northern Ireland and Iraq.
E: richardgoss99@gmail.com

SARA SPIVEY
Sara spent a number of years working in marketing, training, and business communications in the West End, London. She was lucky enough to receive some of the best training facilities on a monthly basis, covering many aspects, including training to train, presentation techniques, negotiating, public speaking, counselling, coaching, budgeting, forecasting, and critical and lateral thinking with full motivation and leadership skills. After this she moved to Hong Kong as the first female Associate VP for ESPN to run the APAJ region managing the top 20 global advertisers from Nike to Coke. She fell In love with the Far East and the emerging artwork scene. So when she relocated to Phoenix, Arizona in 2000 she started her own business. This she did, becoming an independent art dealer specialising in Vietnamese painting and Chinese sculptures which was well received in the US and European markets, with some of the most renowned artist and galleries, with pieces often in the millions of dollars across

the markets. This included the full running of PR, news interviews, television interviews and newspaper articles; supporting artists and promoting their work. After spending ten years in America she moved to the Middle East and returned to Europe to pursue training and education, where she developed soft and business skills for corporates and individuals, together with teaching English language and English for Business at international schools, and Cambridge exam centres for their level of training, invigilating and exam procedures recognised worldwide. She is currently teaching English and Business at LUISS University, Rome. She is also a published author; having a novel, four compilations and four short stories published through her publisher in London.
E: sara_sparky@email.com

SARAH CLARKE

Writing on issues she is passionate about, in the spring of 2018 UK national and resident of Bahrain, Sarah began to explore subjects such as mental health, inclusion and sustainability through the interplay of words and art. Suicide in Bahrain is on the rise, particularly among marginalised communities. Sarah's first published and illustrated poem focuses on the invisible turmoil and distress experienced by the isolated across all segments of society; crises that become visible to those who have the courage to ask before thoughts are acted upon.
E: sfclarke321@gmail.com
Instagram: @sarahclarke888

SHEREEN ABRAHAM

Shereen is an artist, writer, life coach, clinical hypnotherapist, Pranic healer and devotee of all things creative. Born and raised in India, she moved to the Middle East in the late 1990s. A post-graduate in Marketing Management, she was part of the corporate world for several years in varied industries, both in India and the Middle East. Shereen believes; *Experience is one of life's best teachers*, and *Colours are therapeutic*. She finds inspiration in the life that surrounds her… simple things like music, the sights, sounds and smell of nature, the colours and aroma of food, people and their fleeting emotions. She is passionate about everything she does or chooses to do. For her it's important that the journey is as exciting as the destination.
E: shereen.abraham@gmail.com
FB: @ShereenAbrahamArt
Instagram: @shereenabrahamart

SUE THOMASON
Sue was born in 1956 and is still writing.
E: suethomason@myphone.coop

TRISHA LAWTY
E: trishlawty@yahoo.co.uk

ZAHRA ZUHAIR
At 27 years of age, Zahra has grown as an artist, having studied and written numerous pieces, most of which is poetry. In her work, she explores themes of mental health, society and socio politics, and faith in God. She credits her talent to her own mental well-being, and is often seeking opportunities to expand her talent as a writer. She is interested in a diverse range of subjects; from International Relations to creative thinking, and is drawn towards subjects and fields that allow her to create products of significance or to act towards goals for self-fulfilment or the betterment of society, and people around her. As a writer and an academic, she questions norms and conformity, and often thinks about possibilities of alternate realities.
E: zahrazuhair.91@gmail.com
FB: @zahra.zuhair.39
Blog: www.keeeptalking.wordpress.com
LinkedIn: @zahra-zuhair-5476a190

HELP

Groups and organisations worldwide offering support and help to people in crisis and thinking about taking their own life.

AUSTRALIA

LIFELINE

A national charity providing all Australians experiencing a personal crisis with access to 24 hour crisis support and suicide prevention services. We're committed to empowering Australians to be suicide-safe through connection, compassion and hope. Our vision is for an Australia free of suicide.
W: www.lifeline.org.au
T: 13 11 14

SAMARITANS

We understand that sometimes we can feel helpless or lost, especially when feeling overwhelmed, isolated or disconnected from others. We also believe that everyone has the capacity to find their inner strength and resilience. Our volunteers are trained to provide a safe and caring support environment to help you explore your feelings, and uncover your options for a pathway forward.
W: www.thesamaritans.org.au
T: 135 247

CANADA

DISTRESS CENTRE OF OTTAWA AND REGION

Working within the continuum of mental health services, the Distress Centre of Ottawa and Region contributes to a healthier and safer community by providing suicide prevention, crisis intervention, psychological stabilization, emotional support, information, referral and education services, without judgement, to individuals in need.
W: www.dcottawa.on.ca/

SUICIDE ACTION MONTRÉAL

Offering Montrealers who are either witnesses, distressed, worried or bereaved, a range of support services to help them through their problems. Our services also cover the support and formation of crisis workers and organisations iinvolved or touched by suicide.
W: www.suicideactionmontreal.org/en/
T: 1 866 277 3553

HONG KONG

SAMARITANS HONG KONG
Because we know emotional distress does not discriminate or choose its time, we are always here for our callers, 24 hours a day, 365 days a year. Because suicide continues to be one of the leading causes of death in Hong Kong, we have to do as much as we can, despite limited resources, to raise emotional health awareness and to encourage people in need to seek emotional support.
W: www.samaritans.org.hk
T: 2896 0000

SUICIDE PREVENTION SERVICES
Supporting people who are suicidal, despairing or distressed by means of befriending and other services, supporting them to regain control of their emotions and the will to live on. We also aim at raising general awareness towards suicide and identifying ways in which suicide can be effectively addressed.
W: www.sps.org.hk
T: 2382 0000

NEW ZEALAND

SAMARITANS (New Zealand)
Providing confidential emotional support 24/7 to those experiencing loneliness, depression, despair, distress or suicidal feelings. Whatever you're going through, call us any time.
W: www.samaritans.org.nz
T: 0800 726 666

SINGAPORE

SAMARITANS (Singapore)
As one of the only 24-hour hotlines in Singapore, we provide round the clock emotional support for those in distress. This service is manned by trained volunteers.
W: www.sos.org.sg
T: 1800-221 4444

SRI LANKA

SUMITHRAYO (Sri Lanka)
At Sumithrayo we provide Confidential Emotional Support for people who are experiencing, feelings of distress or despair, including those

that may lead to suicide.
W: www.sumithrayo.org
T: 011 2692909

UNITED KINGDOM

CALM
The Campaign Against Living Miserably (CALM) is leading a movement against male suicide, the single biggest killer of men under 45 in the UK.
W: www.thecalmzone.net
T: 0800 585858

CHILDLINE
Childline is here to help anyone under 19 in the UK with any issue they're going through. You can talk about anything. Whether it's something big or small, our trained counsellors are here to support you. Childline is free, confidential and available any time, day or night.
W: www.childline.org.uk
T: 0800 1111

LIFELINE (N.Ireland)
For anyone in N.Ireland who is in distress or despair. Immediate help on phone 24 hours a day 7 days a week. Face to face counselling can be arranged, also befriending, mentoring. Issues dealt with include suicide prevention, self harm, abuse, trauma, depression, anxiety.
W: www.lifelinehelpline.info
T: 0808 808 8000

MIND
We're Mind, the mental health charity. We won't give up until everyone experiencing a mental health problem gets both support and respect. We can help you make choices about treatment, understand your rights or reach out to sources of support.
W: www.mind.org.uk
T: 029 2039 5123
E: supporterrelations@mind.org.uk

PAPYRUS
The national charity dedicated to the prevention of young suicide.Our vision is for a society which speaks openly about suicide and has the resources to help young people who may have suicidal thoughts.
W: www.papyrus-uk.org
T: 0800 068 41 41

Text: 0778 620 9697
E: pat@papyrus-uk.org

PREMIER LIFELINE

The National Christian Helpline is a confidential telephone helpline offering a listening ear, emotional and spiritual support from a Christian perspective, prayer and signposting. Open 9am to midnight every day of the year.
W: www.premierlifeline.org.uk
T: 0300 111 0101

SAMARITANS

Whatever you're going through, a Samaritan will face it with you. We're here 24 hours a day, 365 days a year. Call 116 123 for free.
W: www.samaritans.org
T: 116 123

THE SILVER LINE

The Silver Line is the only free confidential helpline providing information, friendship and advice to older people, open 24 hours a day, every day of the year.
W: www.thesilverline.org.uk
T: 0800 4 70 80 90

UNITED STATES OF AMERICA

HOPELINE

HopeLine, Inc. is an independent volunteer organization originally founded by a group of concerned local citizens providing a confidential telephone service for people in crisis.
W: www.hopeline-nc.org

IMALIVE

A service of the Kristin Brooks Hope Center (KBHC), a non-profit organization. Our focus is suicide intervention, prevention, awareness and education. We provide help and hope through online crisis chat, college campus and high school events and other educational programs.
W: www.imalive.org

INTERNATIONAL ASSOCIATION FOR SUICIDE PREVENTION

Dedicated to: preventing suicidal behaviour, alleviating its effects, and providing a forum for academics, mental health professionals, crisis workers, volunteers and suicide survivors. If you are feeling suicidal or know of someone who needs help, browse HELP on the

IASP website to find a crisis centre anywhere in the world.
W: www.iasp.info

NATIONAL SUICIDE PREVENTION LIFELINE
We can all help prevent suicide. The Lifeline provides 24/7, free and confidential support for people in distress, prevention and crisis resources for you or your loved ones, and best practices for professionals.
W: www.suicidepreventionlifeline.org
T: 1 800 273 8255

SAFE HELPLINE
Safe Helpline offers free, anonymous, confidential, and secure support 24/7. For US DoD Military Service members.
W: www.safehelpline.org
T: 877-995-5247

SUICIDE.ORG
Suicide is NEVER the answer, getting help is the answer. If you are suicidal, have attempted suicide, or are a suicide survivor, you will find help, hope, comfort, understanding, support, love, and extensive resources here.
W: www.Suicide.org

If you are a charity or organisation anywhere in the world offering help and support for people in crisis, and wish to be listed on our website, please go to: www.suicidethebook.com/help/

SUICIDE 2 – More poetry and short prose from writers around the world on the themes of suicide and self-harm.

"Because I have had so many people from around the world wanting to write about these very important themes, I shall be compiling a second edition shortly, so if you missed the deadline for this title, but would like to write a piece or pieces about the above topics, then please contact me.

"You can be a complete novice, with little or no writing experience, or a seasoned writer with many titles to your credit, and you can write about anything to do with the themes of suicide and self-harm, from either your own thoughts, feelings and personal experiences - past or present - or about the experiences of friends, family and people close to you. You can, of course, write under your real name or a pseudonym. Non-fictional contributions only please.

"For further details, deadlines and submission terms & conditions please contact me."

ROBIN BARRATT – Editor/Publisher
E: RobinBarratt@hotmail.com
W: www.RobinBarratt.co.uk/Contribute

EROS - A Collection of Poetry and Prose on Desire and the Erotic

The TENTH in the Collections of Poetry and Prose book series.

With many of the contributions reflecting the diverse backgrounds and cultures of the writers, in EROS there are 97 contributions from 42 writers in 17 countries: Australia, Bahrain, Canada, Egypt, England, Greece, Kenya, Malta, Nepal, Nigeria, Pakistan, Poland, Republic of Ireland, Scotland, South Africa, Switzerland and the USA, all exploring the themes of desire - sexual or romantic - lust, attraction, sexual fantasy and carnal longing.

From both the emerging novice and the established professional, EROS is a unique collection of poetry and short prose from some of the most talented and inspirational writers around the world.

Paperback £9.99 (GBP). ISBN: 978-1718635227
Kindle £3.99 (GBP). ASIN: B07G5FMK89

THE ELEMENTS - A Collection of Poetry and Prose on Earth, Air, Water and Fire

The NINTH in the Collections of Poetry and Prose book series.

With topics including; earthquakes, nature, volcanos, forests, storms, floods, the sea, drought, tsunami, tornados, snow, pollution, desert and many others, in The ELEMENTS there are 122 contributions from 50 writers in 19 countries: Australia, Bahrain, Brazil, Canada, China, England, India, Ireland, Italy, Kenya, Malawi, Malta, New Zealand, Pakistan, Poland, Scotland, South Africa, Switzerland and the USA, all exploring the themes of earth, air, water and fire.

From both the emerging novice and the established professional, The ELEMENTS is a unique collection of poetry and short prose from some of the most talented and inspirational writers around the world.

Paperback £9.99 (GBP). ISBN: 978-1986441209
Kindle £3.99 (GBP). ASIN: B07D61JBD9

EMPOWERMENT - A Collection of Poetry and Prose on Personal Growth & Empowerment

The EIGHTH in the Collections of Poetry and Prose book series.

With topics including finding love, womanhood, illness and disease, overcoming poverty and prejudice, running the marathon, combatting fear, forgiveness, fighting abuse, and many others, in EMPOWERMENT there are 85 contributions from 45 writers in 19 countries: Australia, Bahrain, Canada, China, England, Greece, India, Kenya, Malaysia, Malta, New Zealand, Nigeria, Pakistan, Poland, Scotland, South Africa, Switzerland, Tanzania and the USA, all exploring the themes of empowerment and personal growth.

EMPOWERMENT is a unique collection of poetry and short prose from some of the most talented and inspirational writers around the world.

Paperback £9.99 (GBP). ISBN: 978-1981797349
Kindle £3.99 (GBP). ASIN: B07B9ML43K

THE SEASONS – A Collection of Poetry and Prose on Spring, Summer, Autumn and Winter

The SEVENTH in the Collections of Poetry and Prose book series.

With many of the contributions reflecting the diverse backgrounds and cultures of the writers, in THE SEASONS there are 119 contributions from 46 writers in 19 countries: Australia, Bahrain, Canada, England, Greece, India, Italy, Malawi, Malaysia, Malta, New Zealand, Northern Ireland, Republic of Ireland, Scotland, South Africa, Sri Lanka, Tanzania, USA and Vietnam, all exploring the seasons – spring, summer, autumn and winter - in their particular country or location.

THE SEASONS is a unique collection of poetry and short prose from some of the most talented and inspirational writers around the world.

Paperback £9.99 (GBP). ISBN: 978-1546891161
Kindle £3.99 (GBP). ASIN: B074JFSPSH

BETRAYAL - A Collection of Poetry and Prose on Betrayal and Being Betrayed

The SIXTH in the Collections of Poetry and Prose book series.

BETRAYAL not only covers emotional betrayal and infidelity, but betrayal at work, in health, at war, with life and the betrayal of addiction.

With many of the contributions reflecting the diverse backgrounds and cultures of the writers, in BETRAYAL there are 128 contributions from 60 writers in 24 countries; Antigua, Australia, Bahrain, Bhutan, Canada, England, Greece, India, Japan, Kenya, Malawi, Malaysia, Malta, Mexico, New Zealand, Nigeria, Poland, Republic of Ireland, Scotland, South Africa, Sri Lanka, Tanzania, USA and Vietnam, all exploring the themes of betrayal and being betrayed.

BETRAYAL is a unique collection of poetry and short prose from some of the most talented and inspirational writers around the world.

Paperback £9.99 (GBP). ISBN: 978-1545417737
Kindle £3.99 (GBP). ASIN: B071WG36FW

HAPPY - A Collection of Poetry and Prose on Happiness and Being Happy

The FIFTH in the Collections of Poetry and Prose book series.

What makes people happy? What is happiness? Can happiness be found from people, places and things around us, or is it purely internal – a reflection and result of our own thoughts, feelings, attitude and mindset? Can we really be as happy as we want to be?

With many of the contributions reflecting the diverse backgrounds and cultures of the writers, in HAPPY there are 129 contributions from 60 writers in 21 countries: Antigua, Australia, Bahrain, Canada, England, France, Greece, Indonesia, Ireland, Kenya, Malaysia, Mexico, New Zealand, Nigeria, Puerto Rica, Scotland, South Africa, Sri Lanka, Uganda, USA and Vietnam, all exploring themes of happiness and being happy.

HAPPY is a unique collection of poetry and short prose from some of the most talented and inspirational writers around the world.

Paperback £9.99 (GBP). ISBN: 978-1542482264
Kindle £3.99 (GBP). ASIN: B06XDQPG38

WAR - A Collection of Poetry and Prose on the Bravery and Horror of War

The FOURTH in the Collections of Poetry and Prose book series.

With many of the contributions reflecting the diverse backgrounds and cultures of the writers, in WAR there are 170 contributions from 77 writers in 29 countries as diverse as Bahrain and Bolivia, England and India.

Covering the two World Wars, the wars in the Middle East, Africa and Asia, conflicts in the Balkans, Eastern Europe and Ireland, as well as historical wars, war in general, PTSD, the side-effects of war and much, much more... WAR - A Collection of Poetry and Prose on the Bravery and Horror of War is a thought-provoking, moving and often harrowing, yet also occasionally heart-warming and uplifting collection of poetry and short prose from some of the most talented and inspirational writers around the world.

Paperback £9.99 (GBP). ISBN: 978-1539565888
Kindle £3.99 (GBP). ASIN: B01N6NETRR

TRAVEL - A Collection of Poetry and Prose on Travels and Travelling

The THIRD in the Collections of Poetry and Prose book series.

From a bleak bus ride through Glasgow at midnight, to a trans - Californian road trip, from summer in Dubrovnik and finding peace in a Spanish paradise, to a bumpy bus ride to Kampala and the Paris Metro at night... TRAVEL, the third of the Collections of Poetry and Prose book series, features 97 contributions from 46 writers and poets around the world, all writing in their own unique, wonderful and occasionally quirky way about their travels and experiences travelling.

TRAVEL explores the world and its people and culture in an undeniably unique and fascinating way.

Paperback £9.99 (GBP). ISBN: 978-1535080767
Kindle £3.99 (GBP). ASIN: B01M2WZJIA

LOVE - A Collection of Poetry and Prose on Loving and Being in Love

The SECOND in the Collections of Poetry and Prose book series.

LOVE - A Collection of Poetry and Prose on Loving and Being in Love features 194 contributions from 86 writers and poets around the world, all writing in their own unique, wonderful and occasionally quirky way about loving and being in love.

From rural towns and villages in Africa, Asia and India, and the tiny islands of Bahrain and Shetland, to the bustling metropolises of Europe, the Americas and Australasia, with an eclectic mixture of both traditional and modern verse, as well as the more abstract and esoteric, and with many of the contributions reflecting the diverse backgrounds and cultures of the writers, *LOVE* is being praised worldwide for its diversity and mix of poets, writers and styles.

Paperback £9.99 (GBP). ISBN: 978-1532701726
Kindle £3.99 (GBP). ASIN: B01HWDINB0

LONELY - A Collection of Poetry and Prose on Loneliness and Being Alone

The FIRST in the Collections of Poetry and Prose book series.

Featuring 118 contributions from 57 writers in 26 countries, with many of the contributions reflecting the diverse backgrounds and cultures of the writers, and all writing in their own unique style, *LONELY - A Collection of Poetry and Prose on Loneliness and Being Alone*, is an extraordinary, unique and eclectic mixture of both traditional and modern verse, and short prose, from writers around the world.

Focusing on just about every aspect of loneliness and being alone, and covering topics as diverse as old age, bereavement, abandonment, divorce, entrapment, unrequited love, depression, trauma, failure and addiction, as well as the more abstract and esoteric, *LONELY* has been acclaimed worldwide for its diversity and mix of writers and styles.

Paperback £9.99 (GBP). ISBN: 978-1523912780
Kindle £3.99 (GBP). ASIN: B01DQLHF70

www.RobinBarratt.co.uk

Printed in Great Britain
by Amazon